Editor, MARY BROOKS PICKEN

The Spirit of Service

An Idea

Sometimes, when you are sewing a seam, making a bed, or creaming a cake, an idea strikes you and you wish you had someone to tell it to, some one to share it with, some one to approve of it.

Years ago, a school teacher in Arcadia, Kansas, gave lessons in crocheting, and every Saturday morning her nine pupils gathered in a little hotel parlor for instruction. I learned to crochet in this class. I made a pair of baby bootees out of black yarn. I could not afford to buy outright pink or blue or white, so for practice the left-over black ball of Grandma's had to serve the purpose. But even though the yarn was black, I wanted to make the little bootees for my small brother. I remember quite definitely how painstakingly I worked and how I tried to write down "chain 8, shell 6, and turn," etc. I was the youngest in the class and often had to wait for instruction, so I felt, as a result, that I lost much time.

A Contact

As the years passed and I searched and hunted for information, trying out every interesting thing that I found advertised or that I heard about, I realized more and more how difficult it was to get authentic information. I remember one time trying to develop a yellow-and-black silk pillow from a newspaper description. I bought the material, worried and worked with it, and finally gave up, humiliated and disappointed. And I tried many times afterward to follow written instructions because the idea always appealed to me and seemed worth while. Many times I was successful, many times disappointed, but the thought was continually in mind.

And then came the opportunity to work out for the Woman's Institute the plan that had been growing through the years. The textbooks in dressmaking were prepared, Dorothy Harmeling enrolled as the first one to study them, and then many more came, until there are nearly a hundred students each week graduating in Woman's Institute Courses.

The desire, the opportunity, and then the student contact. All these have been essentially vital in the achievements of the Institute, but the contact by letter and the work accomplished by and with students have made growth and permanence and security.

Our students are our best critics, our best helpers. They tell us when things are bad and when they are good. Every complaint from a student is carefully recorded so that we may avoid a similar situation or supply what is desired and thus make the path easier for the next student. Our new courses, their virtues, their improvements, are due largely to students' suggestions and criticisms

A Birthday

The Woman's Institute celebrates its eighth birthday this month. Emerson has so fitly said, " 'Tis the spirit of greatness that builds institutions that deal with humanities." From the first, the Institute has been blessed with two fountains of greatness, which have poured out, in bountiful measure, enthusiasm, interest, loyalty, and substantial help, and these two sources are the wonderful student body and the Institute staff itself. Few individuals by themselves are great, but working together they attain a strength that truly works miracles. My mother often said, when we children had a problem, "Remember, the Bible says that when two or more of you are of the same mind and work together, great good may be accomplished."

And this surely explains the growth and progress the Institute has made during these past eight years. Students and teachers have worked together in achieving a happy goal; so it is the *Spirit of Service* that celebrates its birthday rather than the Institute itself.

The Spirit of Service

We are hoping for a greater tomorrow in the Woman's Institute. The desire is prevalent everywhere to serve the mother so well today that she will send us her daughter tomorrow. And so, with such an aim, we hope the growth will be substantial and permanent, something of which every one of us may be proud.

So let us all—students, graduates, and staff members—link hands in celebrating happily this Birthday, and pledge ourselves anew to the cause that is helping women everywhere to partake of the Spirit of Service that builds permanently and well.

Good Taste in Dress

And a *Simple* Plan for *Achieving* It

By MARY BROOKS PICKEN

Director of Instruction

SOME say that a woman, in order to hold the affections of a man, must possess to a large degree at least two of the three great essentials—mental, spiritual, and physical beauty. Not all women can be really beautiful, but every woman can acquire a right mental attitude and a spiritual charm that will make up for any lack of physical attractiveness. And it is entirely possible to intensify these two wonderful qualities of mental strength and spiritual dignity by proper grooming, by a close watch for what is becoming and pleasing, and then by an even more careful avoidance of garments and styles that should not be worn. Every woman, if she decides to do it and will work hard enough at it, can express to a pleasing, if not a delightful, degree the three charms of woman.

If we have a diamond, we keep it clean and polished; if we have silver, we keep it bright and shining; if we have windows, we keep them washed so that they will be just as bright and clear as possible. Why not be just as interested in taking care of ourselves? Being mentally alert by contact with people, we can keep the windows of our mind as bright and clear as those of our homes. Going to church, doing good, thinking kindly thoughts, helping others—all will help in developing within ourselves a sense of the spiritual bond that exists in all mankind. And then, by study, we can work to express as intelligently as possible the lovely Bess or Mary or Jane that we want our friends and loved ones to see.

SOME women think that, because they are large and ill-proportioned, they should not dress up, that plain house dresses are best for them. But incorrect proportions only mean understanding them and then working to conceal them.

A few months ago, a lovely lady came to see me. I was amazed when she told me that she weighed two hundred and seventy pounds. She wore a dark blue dress with beautiful hand-made collar and cuffs of net and lace; her hat was shiny black; and her gloves were white. She was so immaculately groomed and had so much personal attractiveness that I entirely forgot her size. I admired her because she had made the very most of her good features and had done it so well that I was entirely unconscious of any handicaps that she, no doubt, had worked to conceal.

In decided contrast, I saw recently a group of women who were a great disappointment to me. Some wore high shoes that had not been polished for a long time, with flimsy silk dresses of bright color. I saw, too, velvet hats that had seen both dust and rain, draggly feathers, gloves that needed mending and cleaning, dresses that were too big or too little, colors that emphasized lack of clear-

ness of complexion, hair that was heavy and lusterless—all things that made these women very drab and unattractive.

To know how splendid some of these women are, it would be necessary to talk to them, to see them in their homes with their children, and to find the kindly soul of each, which, when in evidence, would overshadow the unattractiveness of the exterior. When I saw these women, I felt that I should like to take each one as an individual and help her, if I could, to see her own good points and to bring them out. But as these were not

A Half Dozen Rules

FIRST: Aim always to be refreshingly clean and carefully groomed.

SECOND: Consider what is becoming to you as an individual. If you are not sure, study and experiment until you find out what you can and cannot wear.

THIRD: When you know what is becoming, try to achieve becomingness in an attractive way, emphasizing as much "smartness" in dress as age, circumstances, and occasion will allow.

FOURTH: For surety, make a definite rule to assemble your attire and decide on every detail before you start to dress.

FIFTH: When you are dressed, look yourself over carefully in front of your mirror and improve every detail as much as possible. Before the last look or the last dab of powder, consider carefully whether you are overdressed and whether all accessories go together, and especially make certain that you are not overtrimmed with jewelry, necklaces, or knickknacks.

SIXTH: Then, when all is done, put on a smile that expresses the finest that is in you, that compliments you for doing your best. And if, to this smile, you add all the kindliness that you can command, all the happiness that you can summon, your friends and your very own folks will declare you charming.

Institute students, I could not be so free with them as I might with those who really expect me to help them.

BUT there is a way to appear rightly dressed and there are quite definite rules for every one to apply. First, we should avoid everything that is gaudy and unbecoming, and then strive for cleanliness and freshness of appearance, working all the while so interestingly at the task that it will be impossible to wear "unshined shoes and draggly hats."

One woman whom I know and who looks like a fashion plate in the day time and like a dream lady at night, always gets everything together on the bed before she starts to dress. She insists that it takes only a little longer to do this, that it saves time when she does get ready to dress, and that she is always better satisfied with the results. She says, "I know then that I have the right slip, the right stockings, that my gloves are suitable, and that there are no holes that need attention. In putting them on the bed, I always make all the little repairs that are necessary and do all the brushing or freshening that is needed; then when I am ready to dress I feel a sense of satisfaction that I can find in no other way."

AND so, why don't *you*, who are striving to express yourself more beautifully, to dress with more satisfaction and peace of mind, try this simple little plan of thinking about what you are going to wear and getting it ready before you start to dress? Then, watching always what you see in your mirror, your fashion books, on the streets, and in the shops, you will find that which is appropriate, becoming, and wholly lovely for you.

And to these material fundamentals, add your own wholesome pride. Don't cheat yourself or those who must see you. Don't be dowdy. Life is too short and too real for that. Learn to be proud of yourself and dress so that even you will feel a sense of security and assurance. After all, we can be rather selfish about just looking nice. Other folks are glad to see us in pretty clothes—looking our best. A right hat, a right dress, correctly worn, can really do wonders as a tonic. Try it. It truly is a good prescription.

Smart *Tailleurs* Herald *Spring*

By MARY MAHON
Department of Millinery

As a complement to the spring suits, the hats that all knowing Parisians have pronounced the mode and that are now having their premier show at the winter resorts, are characterized by a strictly tailored note.

While the general trend of shapes is toward the small and close-fitting type, considerable interest is being centered in the crowns, which are narrower in effect and much higher than they have been for some time. The sugar-loaf variety, that is, the high and dome-like crown, is supplanting the regulation balloon effect of the past several seasons.

These new crowns are divided into many sections and in the most unusual ways as well. The sections this season are of horizontal inclination r a t h e r than vertical, as of last, each separately piped and varying in size so that they sometimes appear to be uneven. In some instances, also, the sections are more curved than previously.

There is a wealth of inspiration in the new fabrics, for every kind of hair and visca weave is used, these often being fitted suavely over rolled and cornered brims. Among the most noteworthy allovers are novelty haircloths in leghorn weave; hemp hand-crocheted with a tinsel thread; grosgrain-straw fabric, which requires no frame and is considered the best new allover of its sort; colorful Turkish toweling; imprimé kid, which resembles sea-weed; cretonne appliqué; and brocaded duvetyn.

Although every indication points to the fact that we are at the beginning of a vogue for plaids and stripes, nothing can surpass the smartness of black for chic, tailored wear, because there are so many interpretations of all black; such as, the dull black of crêpe and some straws, the gloss of satin, and the sheen of ciré. Then, too, there are the embossed and raised materials in black that have both lights and shadows in their patterns.

The combination of two colors instead of tones, as in the past season, is another mark of distinctiveness in the coming season. In brown, the new Mexico, a sort of henna or brick, is most popular, and combined with lariat, the new bisque, or light beige, is very effective. Blues are bounding forth in their true fashion. Sapphire, royal, and quantities of copen, now called Empire, are found in every display. Chinese red and the more subdued lacquer are strong factors, too. But most attractive in the new coloring is the exquisite range called sunshine shades. From the soft, pale yellow to orange, and from the bamboo to the new sunkist hues, these rare color combinations find many admirers when design and artistry are the chief consideration.

The simplicity of the line in these tailored models is emphasized in the trimming. Bar and double-end pins are used, while jewels of all colors are attached by means of metal thread. And now comes the metal "clou," or nail head, from Paris to replace our glass beads. Smartest of all trimming novelties is the brilliant, cut steel, or

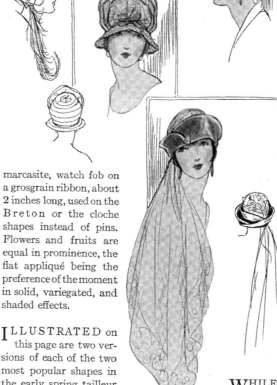

marcasite, watch fob on a grosgrain ribbon, about 2 inches long, used on the Breton or the cloche shapes instead of pins. Flowers and fruits are equal in prominence, the flat appliqué being the preference of the moment in solid, variegated, and shaded effects.

Illustrated on this page are two versions of each of the two most popular shapes in the early spring tailleur collection; namely, the cloche and the turban that is smoothly fitted and creased rather than draped or twisted, as formerly. Slashed and double-effect coronets characterize these new turbans, which are shaped to give a crosswise curve rather than a long back-to-front line.

This feature is evidenced in the model at the upper left, which is a close tricorne shape, the coronet slashed in the front and at the sides and partly concealing a rather high dome crown made of allover black haircloth. The coronet is fitted severely plain with the haircloth, the edge being bound with No. 5 black grosgrain ribbon. The crown is covered in two pieces; a circular tip and a bias side piece that has its top edge bound with the ribbon.

A long, question-mark feather of burnt pheasant tails in dark brown is attached to the side crown at the right side and extends low over the shoulder. Other trims, however, may be substituted if this type is not appropriate and becoming.

Navy and black is the color combination of the model illustrated at the center and developed of starched cotton lace or fancy hair or novelty visca braid. This is an entirely frameless hat, but a 2-inch-wide cloche brim with a high dome crown is needed as a foundation guide.

To make the brim, place one layer of maline over the foundation brim and pin around the edge. Sew the first row of lace or braid around the edge and continue spirally into the head-size. Stitch through the maline, but not through the frame, and attach to a No. 7 ribbon-wire head-size band. Steam thoroughly, rip open the outer edge, attach a wire around this edge of the braid, and bind with No. 3 black moiré ribbon.

To make the crown, place a layer of maline over a dome crown and pin in small plaits around the base. Beginning at the base, sew the lace or braid spirally, catching it to the maline only. After steaming, unpin the maline from the foundation crown, slip the crown over the head-size of the brim, and stitch secure.

The frameless hat is now ready for the trim, which consists of five rows of the lace or braid bound with black moiré ribbon and sewed in semicircular fashion across the front from side to side. A band of the black ribbon is drawn around the base of the crown and knotted in a single tie-bow in front.

While the leadership of combinations consisting of black and brown, and black and navy, is unquestioned, there is no lack of bright color introduced in solid and changeable effect, as is illustrated in the version of the cloche at the upper right. This visor brim and round crown are covered plain in copen faille, and the coronet, or bulged cuff, is covered with flat-appliqué flower, fruit, and conventional motifs of cut-out felts, suéde, and soutache braid interspersed with gold and silver stitches.

At the lower right, another version of the cuff-brim turban is illustrated. The crown, a high dome, is of black milan straw. Bias, black haircloth covers the coronet-cut brim that folds over in a double effect across the back to the right side so as to allow the lace veil, which is draped over the crown, to come through and fall in a long point over the right shoulder.

Clothes Make The *Man*

(And *Mother* Makes the Clothes)

By CLARICE CARPENTER
Department of Dressmaking

IN this month of hearts and heroes, what could be more appealing to the heart of the small hero of the household than the manly little garments here pictured? They have their appeal to Mother, too, for each is simple to make and most of them are washable as well.

Boys, you know, have just as big a streak of vanity in their make-up as do girls; it merely expresses itself in a different form. While a girl is very particular about her frills and plaits, her small brother is priding himself no less in his rather exaggerated air of nonchalance. He will tell you that he doesn't care *what* he looks like. But let Mother put a frill on the blouse of a boy past three or four, or use velvet in making a suit, and the result is likely to be nothing short of a riot. Clothes then loom on his horizon with enormous proportions, for he knows he has been put in a position to be greatly embarrassed by the remarks of his fellows.

So, Mother, in planning your son's spring wardrobe, remember that he will think you are just the most understanding person in all the world if his suits follow very plain, straight lines, imitate to a great degree the corresponding garments in the wardrobe of Father or Big Brother, and always have plenty of pockets.

THE garments illustrated have been chosen because of these very points. Only one shows the feminine touch to any marked degree and that is the dressy little suit of blue serge at the left below, which has frills on the collar and cuffs and the center box-plait. But then, one is still broad-minded enough at three to concede that much to one's Mother, and even take pride in the suit.

The coat and the trousers can be made from a remnant of blue serge or cut from the unworn parts of Dad's suit or Auntie Beth's skirt. The blouse might be of white flaxon or similar cotton fabric, or of pongee. If a pattern is desired, Pictorial Review pattern No. 9401 may be used with slight changes.

DO you know a single boy from four to fourteen who would not take great pleasure in repairing his toy Ford or doing any other "regular fellow" sort of job in a suit like the one at the lower center? It is probably the most popular suit in his wardrobe, for look—it has a belt! What if it is made of the same khaki as the trousers and buckled with a ten-cent store buckle? To him, it savors of the days to come when leather belts with silver buckles are to be as much a part of his life as tops and marbles are now.

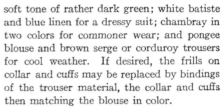

Khaki, as mentioned, is excellent for the trousers. Galatea of the same color is enough lighter in weight to make the little sports type of shirt very comfortable. For days in the schoolroom, where a little more formality is desirable, the sleeves may be long, and the shirt made of madras shirting or chambray and the trousers of any suitable woolen material, such as tweed. Pictorial Review pattern No. 9010 may be used. It comes in sizes 4 to 14.

AT the right below is shown one of the many types of blouses that may be worn either with serge trousers for the early spring days that are still cool, or with trousers of rep, linen, or linen-finished cotton, galatea, or khaki when the days become very warm.

A little suit of this type has endless possibilities for the small boys of three or four years. Various color and fabric combinations may be worked out. The collar and cuffs may be made from scraps left from the trousers, which, by the way, being cut with side seams, might be made from short lengths left in the scrap bag.

Several excellent combinations are cream or ecru soisette blouse with rep trousers in a soft tone of rather dark green; white batiste and blue linen for a dressy suit; chambray in two colors for commoner wear; and pongee blouse and brown serge or corduroy trousers for cool weather. If desired, the frills on collar and cuffs may be replaced by bindings of the trouser material, the collar and cuffs then matching the blouse in color.

A pattern that is somewhat similar to this design is Pictorial Review pattern No. 1584. By pinning the vest pattern onto the front-section pattern and cutting all in one section, it may be adapted to this design.

SEASONS come and go, but the middy belongs to them all. It possesses several characteristics that make for this popularity, not the least of which is its appeal to the imagination of the small boy. Dressed in it, he immediately becomes a sailor, and as such is ready for any adventure as he sails his small boat in the bath tub or the garden pond. Then, too, the middy is very comfortable and is made of very durable materials. It has, also, the virtue of being easy to put on and take off, which is a big help to one's mother. It may be made in either wool or cotton materials to suit any season, and the child's love of color may be gratified by the brilliancy of the red tie.

There are various types, with or without yokes. Some are regulation blouse length and button to the trousers. The one here shown is hip length, but may be rolled up if desired. McCall pattern No. 2545, which comes in sizes 4 to 12, will prove a very satisfactory pattern for this blouse, though it gives, also, the sailor's trousers of full length.

DEAR to the heart of any sturdy lad whose age can still be counted on the fingers of one hand, is the little overall suit at the right above.

It is extremely simple and when made of blue or gray denim or chambray, or any stout cotton material, with bindings and pocket of red, it is as attractive as it is useful. The running-stitch sails, which are done with turkey-red thread on the overall proper, transform the pocket into the truest sort of sail boat. This bit of trimming is so simple that it will require not more than five minutes' extra time, and the joy of the wearer will more than repay one for the slight effort. The back, which is cut like the front, buttons on the shoulder. A button under each arm prevents the blouse from pulling out at that point.

With the aid of McCall pattern No. 2765, one can make this garment for a boy of any age from 2 to 6.

Softness of Line for Slender Matrons

By MARGARET MURRIN
Department of Dressmaking

WHILE the subject of clothes is of definite appeal to both maid and matron, yet it sometimes happens that a woman who has passed her middle years transfers her interest from her own problem to that of the younger members of her family. This tendency may be brought about through the apparent neglect of the older woman by those who are engaged in creating new styles, or it may be merely a feeling of "anything will do" produced by her stepping aside in the forward progress of time and allowing the busy world of events to pass by.

Where there is difficulty in finding a becoming and appropriate style for a garment, it is an easy matter to neglect the purchase or construction of the dress, suit, or hat. And when one's clothes are not appropriate for the social side of life, one is likely to grow indifferent. It follows that the possession of a suitable outfit will not only bring out the attractiveness of the wearer, but also help her to enjoy the companionship of her friends to its fullest extent.

The middle-aged or elderly woman of generous proportions is very kindly considered by designers, for she can usually find models in which length of line is emphasized by both cut and trimming. Not so, however, can the slight woman of similar years, as the designs shown rarely combine the softness of outline and the dignity of cut suited to her age.

A YOUTHFUL design may be adjusted, either by some slight change in cutting or by the addition of an accessory that will soften the severity of the style and make it becoming. Such a plan was followed in the dress illustrated at the left. The dainty collar of lace-trimmed Georgette has a great deal to do with the becomingness of the design, although the surplice effect of the waist and the cut of the skirt are excellent features, too. The former helps to blend waist and skirt together, while the latter will give a slenderizing effect through the hips, which are sometimes large in proportion to the rest of the figure.

Another advantage of this model is that its simplicity makes it appropriate for daily wear, although it can be kept exclusively for dress-up occasions, if desired. Such a dress made up of Canton crêpe in dark blue or black with the collar of cream color, will give excellent service. Other fabrics suitable are wool crêpe, challis, and, for summer, a firm voile or soft-finished lawn.

McCall Pattern 3157 will provide a guide for cutting.

FOR a cloth dress, which is almost a necessity in cool weather, the center design is a suitable style. It may be developed in serge, wool crêpe, or a light-weight wool velour, and

the edges of the collar may be bound with silk braid, while the jabot should be cut from batiste or net. The frill may be trimmed with lace, or it may be finished with a ½-inch hem or a picot edge.

The way in which the cloth collar is applied and the arrangement of the jabot are bound to prove becoming, the latter especially when the figure is flat through the bust. If desired, the material of the jabot could form a collar which would be worn over the one of cloth, particularly if the dark color close to the face would not look well. This extra collar should be cut slightly smaller than the cloth one and should be finished in the same manner as the jabot.

Black Poiret twill with trimming of gray Georgette would make a smart outfit if the skin is fair and the hair that sort of gray to which gray in one's dress is becoming.

For summer wear, such a model might be cut from dull blue or gray linen and have lace-trimmed net for the frill in front. Pictorial Review Pattern No. 1971 duplicates this design.

TO wear when a guest at an afternoon or evening wedding or a dress-up party, the gown at the right might be chosen. Satin is a dignified material, but should be purchased in one of the crêpe weaves, for a soft fabric is necessary in order to bring out the true beauty of the lines of this dress. If chosen in a becoming gray and trimmed with silver lace, the gown would be very rich, but a less dressy combination could be used with equally as charming a finished effect. Gray Canton crêpe with gray Spanish lace or a medium old rose or blue with cream-colored lace would be lovely, or the entire dress may be kept black.

If black is chosen, an interesting plan would be to make the sleeves of Georgette and embroider them in an all-over design with metallic thread.

Color contrast might be introduced in the waist-line ornament, which is made of loops of ribbon folded to simulate petals and attached to a circular foundation.

To make such an ornament, provide about 4 yards of 1-inch ribbon. Form short lengths into flat loops and sew them firmly to a circle of light-weight buckram about 3 inches in diameter. Begin to sew the petals at the outside and finish the center with a few small rosebuds or tiny loops so as to conceal the raw edges of the ribbon. The ribbon used may be as elaborate as one wishes; for instance, silver on a gray and blue dress; black, edged or faced with silver on a black dress; or black faced with a color that would repeat the color of the sleeves.

As a guide in cutting this model, procure Pictorial Review Pattern No. 1313.

THE keynote of all of these styles is a dignified simplicity combining line, color, and material, each in its proper proportion. Line is usually of first importance, for it is the way a gown is cut and trimmed that makes it suited or unsuited to the slight mature woman. If the figure is unusually tall, crosswise lines may be brought into prominence, and if it is very short, lengthwise constructive details and trimming effects should be emphasized. For the average figure, that style of dress in which the outline is soft and inconspicuous is always best.

For practically all types, color comes next. Choose the less definite tones, avoiding harsh reds, blues, and greens. Be careful about brown, too, unless the skin is quite clear and the eyes are brown. However, bright colors may be used as trimming features, it being often found that colors which seem unbecoming for an entire dress will really bring out one's best points if introduced in small quantities. And the contrast thus produced usually has a desirable effect on the feelings of the wearer.

Materials that are stiff in effect, such as organdie or taffeta, while permissible, are not usually a wise choice, for they are too harsh for this type. The fabrics that drape into soft folds are most friendly to the elderly figure.

Youth may be so strikingly dressed as to form a picture without regard to background, but as one grows older it is desirable to choose one's clothes so as to have the color and the material blend with the personality of the wearer and her environment. Then the effect will be a subdued harmony forming an attractive background, as it were, for the gayer, brighter colors of those who take the more active part in the family life.

And So a Party Was Planned

And This is How it Grew

From a letter of Mary Brooks Picken to Jane Thomas--

Here I am in New York—I know it from many unmistakable outward signs—but my heart and my thoughts are still with you, all gathered about that table making plans for our Eighth Anniversary Celebration for February 29th, as we were this morning when I was called away.

Every one was so enthusiastic and seemed to be so full of happy plans that I should have liked to stay with you and help you complete them. But I know all of you Institute folks so well that I am sure the plans as they stand now are "just right." I am eager, however, to know *all* about them, so you must write to me very soon, for I may be detained here for the next few days.

It hardly seems possible that we are preparing for our Eighth Anniversary, but it is good to look back over these eight years that have been so full. Full of work, of course, and yet filled with splendid friends, too, and happy plans and messages of the fresh courage and helpfulness that the Woman's Institute has brought to so many hearts. The work itself seems to stand out with a glory all its own.

A birthday celebration has always meant a great deal to me. Somehow, every birthday seems a call to my heart for a birthday cake and candles, and today it was just as always; so the proposal of a real giant cake with towering candles, which we could share with our students, was a happy one. To "second that motion" seemed a calm way of voicing my opinion, but, as I remember, I made a few more remarks to indicate that it more than met with my favor. And later, when Miss Davis suggested that we leave a space around the great candles for a little taper for each student who takes an active part in the success of the Eighth Anniversary Celebration by bringing in a new member, it seemed as though the whole place was alight with little lively birthday greetings.

By this time, you know about the new Woman's Institute ring that has been designed for our students. The ring was designed some time ago and the model came just before I left. I am sure you have all agreed that these rings will be something to be proud of and that every member should have one. It will, without a doubt, serve in a splendid way to link our members with one another and to form a happy reminder of their association with the Institute. We are sure to have a happy period now, students and employes together, planning to make the Institute proud of us all on February 29th.

From Jane Thomas' report to Mrs. Picken

We were distressed when you had to leave the meeting yesterday. The Eighth Anniversary plans were so much a part of your thoughts that it seemed as though we should not go on without you. But you had given us a number of ideas, and leaving them to us to work out, as you did, made it seem necessary for us to fill up the little chinks in the framework of fancy you had built. Already, the party plans seem to be going at full tilt and everything is running smoothly.

The first step, after the Birthday Cake and candles had been planned, was to make it possible, as you suggested, for every one of our students to carry the news of a $5 discount on all Woman's Institute Courses to any of their friends who wished to join the Institute during the Anniversary Period. Then a gift of one of the beautiful new Woman's Institute rings is to go to every student who helps a friend to enroll during this time.

You knew about the ring, of course, but it was a surprise to all of us when Mr. Sumner showed us the design yesterday. Every one was delighted with it, Mrs. Picken.

It will be a gift that every student will be very proud to receive. My only suggestion was to provide a big supply of rings, for there's not a student who will not make a special effort to own one of them.

The Anniversary Period has been arranged to cover all of January and February. And it has been decided that *every* student, regardless of where she lives, may have a part in the celebration by receiving one of the lovely rings and by having a little taper lighted as a birthday message on February 29th. Then, after the party, a piece of the birthday cake will be sent to all who have introduced a friend as a member of the Woman's Institute during the Anniversary time. This, of course, is as it should be, for the aim of the Institute has always been to serve its students, and the observance of the Eighth Anniversary should be chiefly for students and for all the friends of the students who wish to be members of the Institute.

After the plans were made, to each one was given a part to carry out.

I am to write the invitations to our students and tell them about the party.

Miss Coyle is to order a sufficient supply of the Woman's Institute rings and to have them in readiness when they are to be sent out.

Miss Byrne is to order the big Birthday Cake and the candles.

I'm sure that each of us started immediately after the meeting to make things ready.

From a memo of Mary E. Coyle to Mrs. Picken--

After the meeting a few days ago, I found myself with the task of ordering Woman's Institute rings for all of our students who take part in the Eighth Anniversary Celebration. It was rather a big order that I sent away, as you can realize, but I received a telegram today saying that the order had received attention and that the rings will be made up at once.

I think we have never planned to send out anything from the Institute that means so much in such a happy way as this ring will mean both to the Institute and to every student who plans to have one for her own. The rings are very lovely in themselves, but in addition to this they carry such a store of meaning that to see one or to wear one will suggest only thoughts of service and friendship, of earnest effort, and of thoughtfulness for others—surely this will mean inspiration.

From a note of Sara L. Byrne to Mrs. Picken—

Of course, you know that to me was given the happy privilege of arranging for our Birthday Cake at our meeting a few days ago. At first this cake loomed up in my thoughts like a huge white mountain with a lofty group of great torch-like candles, and to go out to plan and order such an enormous cake seemed a task rather than a pleasure, for it suggested such a big formal thing. And the loving birthday thoughts that should surround it, seemed lost. But then suddenly I remembered the wide smooth space that was to be left around the center for the students' little candles, and one by one, like little stars, I began to see the glimmer of each tiny taper that is to be added later. A glimmer, and then a radiant glow, and finally my snowy mountain of cake was all asparkle with little star-like birthday thoughts.

So, to plan the great cake was no longer a task but a joy. I am sure you will be glad to know that the order has been given to a jolly old baker who has promised to make "the most beautiful cake in the world," and to have it ready and placed in our main hall on February 29th. The baker asked if we were going to have a birthday party for the world, and I told him that was just about the size of it. He entered into the plans with such enthusiasm that I am confident this will be "the most beautiful birthday cake in the world."

From a letter of Mrs. Edith Johnson (a Woman's Institute Student) to Mrs. Picken—

A wonderful letter full of the most jolly birthday plans came from Jane Thomas today, and I've read it a dozen times. I was glad to know that the 29th of February is the Eighth Anniversary day for the Woman's Institute. You folks up there seem to have made me feel that I belong right in front of that Birthday Cake, though I am only one member of the student group. I promise you, however, I am going to be there in spirit, and *my* little candle—more than one, if possible—is going to show that *I* delivered my message of helpfulness and better womanhood to my friends and neighbors.

That's just what the Woman's Institute is doing. It is organizing a bigger, better band of women who can do things in their homes in the right way. The foundation of this world today is, after all, our *homes*. And it's the women who, in their efforts to make the home and the home folks comfortable and to keep the home folks well-dressed, are making this world a good place in which to live. So why shouldn't I bring the word of this splendid training to my friends? That, it seems to me, will be doing the greatest service next to making my *own* home and my *own* family the very best home and the very best citizens that I can possibly make.

Tomorrow, Buddy Boy and I will go over to see Jessie Howard after the other children are off to school. Jessie has ever been my dearest friend and I mean to share the information about my treasured Course with her first. I believe I'll stop to see Miss Wood, too. She asked me some time ago to send her name to the Institute and I never inquired why she hasn't joined. If she knows about the $5 discount that she may have by enrolling this month or next, I know she will realize that she should take advantage of it at once.

From a letter of Jessie Howard to Mrs. Picken—

Mrs. Edith Johnson, who is one of your students, and her dear little baby called today, and I want you to know that while I was happy just to see them, I was made more than happy by the new hope and courage that Edith Johnson gave me in telling me about your Course.

Here I sat this morning with my spirits at their lowest ebb. John just forcing himself out to the office each morning, when he should be away to a different climate to take care of his precious health, hurts me dreadfully, for I know why he *feels* he must go on. Mother is moving in with us tomorrow. Junior needs glasses, the payment on the house is due next month, a notice came that our street will be paved in the spring, and John feels he has to be ready to meet them all.

Well, Edith Johnson has helped me to solve the problem and I'm happy tonight. I never knew how much I have been spending for our clothes until Edith figured it out for me. Why, just on our own things—the four youngsters', my own, and mother's,—we can save a great many dollars in a year if I make them. And, of course, now that mother will be here, I will be able to do some sewing for others, too. So, I can help John in the way that he most needs help.

That's the hope Edith Johnson brought to *me*, if I were to enroll for a Woman's Institute Course. To you, this may be an old story. I know that many women are situated in similar positions to the one in which I find myself, but I wish, Mrs. Picken, there were more good friends like mine to bring the possibilities of your work to every woman who needs it. I sent my application today while she was here. And though the $10 I sent was a precious thing to me, Mrs. Picken, somehow

I can seem to see that little $10 bill coming back to me with a whole flock of little bills hopping joyfully along behind it.

From a note of Mary Brooks Picken to Jane Thomas—

The first Eighth Anniversary enrolment came this morning from Mrs. Jessie Howard of Ohio. A dear, sincere letter full of hope accompanied the Application for Membership, and it has given me much happiness to have Jessie Howard claim us as friends at once. Her first work has been mailed out, and now we will watch for her first report.

Mrs. Howard's enrolment was due to our Mrs. Edith Johnson's recommendation, and Mrs. Johnson's candle was laid aside this morning to have a place of honor on the big Birthday Cake on the 29th of February. Mrs. Johnson's ring, also, was sent. From my heart, I shall send, with every box that carries a Woman's Institute ring out to a student during this Period, the same little message that I breathed for the ring that went out to Edith Johnson today: "May this little circlet link you more securely to your happy mission of noble womanhood. May it ever remind you that what you do to make your home a better home and those who are dear to you bigger and better men and women, counts in the great Master's scheme of events."

From a letter of Edith Johnson to Mrs. Picken—

My beautiful Woman's Institute ring came today! I've had it on only a few hours now, but somehow it seems to have become a real wishing ring already. Jessie Howard called me today to say her first report has been sent and that she has made the baby three pairs of rompers—the first she has ever tried. She says Bobbie is so proud of them and little Betsy Claire has her order in for a new dress. I can just imagine how happy they will be.

But the thing I see that will mean more than all to the Howards is that Jessie herself will be able to have better clothes if she can make them herself. And once a woman begins to realize that she looks well and that her clothes are correct, she seems to gain a new lease on life. Why, once Jessie begins to notice how charming she can look, she is going to lose a bit of that timid air she has. I'll be the happiest woman alive if what I've done will bring comfort to my friend and her little brood. And somehow I know it will.

Here I am dreaming about a thing that's already started, and this is January 15th! Though I need but one candle on the beautiful big Birthday Cake, I intend to see and talk to every one I know who might be interested

A Month of *Merrymaking*

By LAURA MacFARLANE
Department of Cookery

FEBRUARY, the month of red-letter days, so short and fleeting and yet so full of fun and frolic! And to the usual occasions for festivity—Lincoln's Birthday, St. Valentine's Day, and Washington's Birthday—this year gives an extra day to maids forlorn for Leap Year parties and to Woman's Institute students for the celebration of the Institute's Birthday. Surely, this is the Mardi Gras month of the year and should be celebrated in the true spirit of gaiety.

and tiny ones at each place. Candied cherries wired to the trees and garnishing cookies will give a realistic touch.

The patriotic note may be evident in shield-trimmed candle shades and place cards and in dolls dressed as Colonial dames. The hatchet in cardboard may decorate your place cards and your table, and in cookies, may help to make your menu appropriate.

Small silk flags may be inserted in button molds or fastened to cardboard squares by means of sealing wax. And a very unique napkin holder may be made by fastening two cardboard hatchets together with seals. Then a tightly rolled paper napkin may be slipped through the openings.

WOMAN'S INSTITUTE BIRTHDAY

WITH the festivities at their height, along comes the Woman's Institute Birthday as the crowning event of the month. And, as shown here, it offers you novel methods of entertaining your friends and passing on the story of the Institute and its work.

If you are a Dressmaking student, you will, of course be more interested in the table

ST. VALENTINE'S DAY

THROUGHOUT this whole month, the God of Love holds sway, but the crowning event of his visit—St. Valentine's Day—comes about midway. It's not the slightest trouble to give a party in honor of Dan Cupid, for he takes up the reins the minute he arrives and guides the affair to a frolicsome end.

As shown at the lower center, hearts and arrows and Cupids make a most appropriate setting for this frisky little chap. In a large red heart-shaped box, favors for your guests may be placed, and red streamers may run from them to the Cupid place cards. Red hearts and arrows may be scattered over your table and may trim your candle shades, and Kewpie dolls, dressed in crisp organdie dresses and placed here and there, may help Dan Cupid preside. Charming favors are tiny heart-shaped paper parasols.

Hearts may dominate your menu, with heart-shaped timbales for any creamed food you serve, heart-shaped boxes for bonbons or nuts, and heart-shaped sandwiches, cookies, cakes, and ice cream.

shown at the right. Around your dome or center lights, arrange a ruffle of organdie, or even of paper, in the chosen color, and from it suspend streamers, each bearing a letter of the name—Woman's Institute. Use a sewing basket as your centerpiece and hide your favors in it, which, by the way, may be real sewing utensils, such as thimbles, tape measures, emery bags, dressmaker's gauges, cushions, needle cases, button bags, scissors, etc., or these same articles made in paper, some of which are shown in the center below the table. Tiny emery baskets make lovely place favors, and a paper-rose corsage, each rose containing a handy sewing article, is a most suitable as well as charming prize. A doll dressed as a fashion manikin may be your presiding genius, and thimble shades of pin-pricked, silver paper decorate your candles.

A MILLINERY table is not a whit less attractive and just as easy to arrange. An upturned floppy hat, flower trimmed, may conceal your chandelier, and a gaily decorated hat box form your centerpiece. Tiny, matching hat boxes may hold bonbons, or they may be used as receptacles for your ice cream, and your candle shades may carry the hat box idea, too.

A small doll dressed as a midinette and weighed down with a huge hat box makes a charming favor or table decoration. Your place cards may be cardboard hats with a gay feather stuck through each.

WASHINGTON'S BIRTHDAY

IN honoring "The Father of His Country" on his natal day, you have a wealth of material on which to draw, as the patriotic group indicates. If you wish the cherry tree to sound the note of decoration, you may use a fairly good-sized one in the center of your table

Golden Opportunities

Each in Her Own Small *Way*

GIVEN the *will* to do a thing, one always finds a *way* in which to do it. When a busy homekeeper comes face to face with the fact that she must do something to increase the family income or else forego many of the pleasures of life, and perhaps some of its necessities, it behooves her at once to take stock of her assets and her liabilities. Her assets may be turned into money—her liabilities must be done away with, one by one.

The first and most important fact for her to face is that the handiwork or service she offers to the public must be the very best of which she is capable. And when she stops to think that genius is really "the capacity for taking infinite pains," she will realize that it rests with herself whether she will become a genius in her chosen work.

NEEDLEWORK is the choice of many who cannot go outside of their own homes to market their wares. Monograms are used on everything nowadays, from table linen to lingerie, so if you can embroider well you can reap a goodly profit on work of this kind. Samples of your work may be displayed in the leading linen shop of the town, and at the art counters of department stores.

Women's magazines are the best guide as to what is new in the style of lettering and in the method of embroidering monograms. A supply of patterns and of thread with which to develop the designs is necessary; then with a little practice you can fit a design to any space. The prices that may be charged vary in different localities, but you can always be sure of a profitable income when once you have created a market for this work.

NOT every one has the equipment for making comfortables and quilts, nor has every one, in these busy days, the time to devote to work of this kind. Yet this does not alter the fact that few of us ever feel that our supply of soft, fluffy bed coverings is altogether as complete as we would like to have it. There never comes a time when we wouldn't "just love" to have one more attractive comfortable, and there come many times when we just must have a few more—*made* or *bought*.

You can reap a veritable harvest making comfortables and quilts if your work is neat and true. All the equipment you will need is a frame, consisting of four sticks, each about eight feet long and on one edge of which narrow strips of ticking have been tacked, and four clamps for holding the sticks together at the corners. If customers provide their own materials, about $3.00 is a fair price for the making. For quilting in intricate designs, patterns must be provided, this work being charged for at the rate of $1.50 to $2.50 a spool.

It is very easy to advertise work of this kind, as one pleased customer will tell of her "find;" so, almost before you realize it, orders will come thick and fast.

THEN there is the dear little woman who has no special talent or training, perhaps, but who has a "way of her own" with the wee

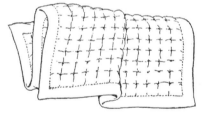

folks. Has it ever occurred to you to capitalize that God-given gift, which too few of us possess? If you live in a section where there are a number of small children, you can make your services a boon to many mothers, for not the least of a busy mother's task is that of shampooing her children's hair. Little tousled heads must be well cared for if the little men and women of tomorrow are to have healthy scalps and thick, luxuriant hair. And work of this kind can easily be done in your own home.

An excellent method of washing a child's hair, one which keeps soapy water from running down little faces and necks, is illustrated here. Just procure a cabinet, a substantial box, or a table of the height of the wash bowl, and place it in the bathroom next to the bowl, as shown. Over the top, place a thick bath mat and under the child's head, a folded Turkish towel. Lay the child on the cabinet in such a position that her head is close to the edge of the bowl, and then proceed to wash her hair, turning her first on one side and then on the other. If the faucets extend far out into the bowl, you may find it necessary to place the stand or table in front rather than at the side of the bowl.

The following recipe makes an excellent shampoo:

2 cakes pure Castile soap
1 cake tar soap
2 qts. water

If the water is hard, add ½ teaspoonful of soda. Also, the tar soap should be omitted for oily heads, and in such cases the quantity of water should be reduced by one pint.

Shave the soap fine and place it in a medium-large kettle. Pour the water on this and boil until the soap is entirely melted. Pour into a jar. Reheat one-half to one pint for each shampoo.

Three to four thorough rinsings are required, depending upon the thickness of the hair—the first rinsing water being warm and the last, luke warm. One-half teaspoonful of lemon juice in the last rinsing water makes blonde hair fluffy and light.

When drying the hair, first massage the scalp with the finger tips and then dry the hair with warm towels.

HAIRCUTTING may be done in connection with shampooing if you have the time to spare for this. The supplies needed include a pair of barber's scissors, two or three good, easily cleaned brushes, and at least two combs, some towels, and a can of unscented talcum powder.

The floor of the room given over to this work should be covered with linoleum or some other washable material. A high chair should be provided for the little ones; one other chair, a rocker, and a dressing table will come in handy, too; and you should, of course, provide toys that may easily be kept clean.

Armed with these few articles and a gracious manner toward the little folks, you may consider yourself well on the high road to success in this interesting work. And all work is interesting if we make it so.

Cake Making—a Real Diversion

By MARY E. COYLE
Director of Correspondence

WOMEN who devote their time to business or to sewing or just to housekeeping, usually have some creative diversion. Personally, I have become greatly interested in cake making, and during my studies and work, I have learned a number of things pertaining to the art of cake making, which I believe will interest some, if not all of you; hence my presumption in presenting a few conclusions as well as some tested recipes.

Because of the limited amount of space, it is necessary to confine my remarks entirely to the butter-cake variety. The making of sponge cake is quite a different process.

CAKE making has been defined as the art of combining flour, sugar, butter, eggs, milk, etc., in such a way as to produce a palatable, delicious, yet nourishing article of food. A lack of knowledge of the "art of combining" has been the cause of many cake failures, even though the proper ingredients have been used.

The best ingredients to be had should be used in a cake, which will place it in the class of luxuries and make it impractical for some families to have cake more than once, or possibly twice, a week. But how much more wholesome and enjoyable it is to have a delicious cake occasionally than to have just ordinary cake every day.

The mixing of a cake should be accomplished as quickly as possible. Cake is never so light and feathery when partly mixed ingredients are allowed to stand for several minutes before others are added.

All ingredients of a cake should be assembled before the mixing is started.

More flour than any other ingredient is used in a cake, and the texture, lightness, and color of the cake depend greatly on the flour used. To secure the best results, a pastry, or cake, flour, which is whiter than bread flour, looks more like starch, feels soft and smooth in the fingers, and holds together when squeezed in the hand, should be used.

SUPPOSE we take a recipe and follow each step carefully. This recipe can be used as a foundation for any layer cake.

½ c. butter	3 tsp. baking powder
1 c. sugar	Pinch of salt
2 eggs	½ tsp. of vanilla
⅔ c. milk	½ tsp. lemon
2 c. flour	

1. Grease two layer-cake tins. Cover only bottom of tin with wax paper, grease again, and set tins aside until they are needed.

2. Sift flour once and then measure 2 cupfuls. Add 3 level teaspoonfuls of baking powder and a pinch of salt, and sift three times. Set aside until needed.

3. Measure 1 cupful of granulated sugar. Roll and sift the sugar until all grains will pass through the sieve. Set aside until needed.

4. Separate the yolks and whites of 2 eggs and set aside in a cool place until needed.

5. Measure ½ cupful of butter and put in a mixing bowl.

6. Measure ⅔ cupful of milk and set aside until needed.

7. Now cream the butter until it is soft and white around the edges. Add the sugar gradually, creaming the mixture meanwhile.

8. Beat the egg yolks until thick and lemon-colored. Add them to the butter-and-sugar mixture. Beat well.

9. Alternate adding a little of the dry ingredients—the flour, baking powder, and salt—and a little of the milk until all are used. Beat the batter hard after each addition of flour and milk.

10. Add the flavoring and beat the batter very hard.

11. Beat the egg whites until stiff but not dry, and carefully fold them into the mixture.

12. Pour the batter into the tins, spreading it high on the sides and at the corners and leaving a slight depression in the center.

13. Bake in a moderate oven from 20 to 30 minutes.

14. When the cake is done, it will shrink from the sides of the tins. It may be tested also by inserting a broom straw in the center. If no particles of dough adhere to the straw, it is done.

15. When cool, the layers may be put together with an icing or a filling and the entire cake then covered with icing.

Secrets of Cake Making

1. Chilled ingredients make the best cakes.
2. Always add a little flour to a butter-and-sugar mixture before adding milk. This will keep the butter from congealing.
3. Sweet milk makes a cake of fine texture. Sour milk makes a tender cake.
4. Brown sugar makes a moist cake.
5. Egg whites will beat more easily if a pinch of salt is added to them.
6. If a boiled icing does not "set" within ten or fifteen minutes after being spread on a cake, put the cake in a slow oven for a very few minutes and it will soon harden.
7. Do not stir sugar and water after it starts to boil. This will make the icing sugary.
8. If icing has been boiled or beaten too long and has a rough appearance on cake, dip a knife in boiling water and spread quickly over the icing several times. This will give a smoother appearance.
9. Egg whites for icing should be beaten stiff; but for the cake they should not be so stiff, or the cake will be dry.
10. Too hot an oven will brown cake on top before it has sufficiently risen. A loaf cake should always be baked in a moderate oven.

Spice Cake

⅔ c. butter	4 tsp. baking powder
1⅓ c. sugar	¼ tsp. salt
3 eggs	1 tsp. nutmeg
1¼ c. milk	1 tsp. cinnamon
3 c. flour	⅓ c. raisins

Sift together the flour, salt, baking powder, and spices. Cream butter, add sugar gradually. Add well beaten eggs. Mix well. Add sifted dry ingredients alternately with the milk. Place two-thirds of the batter in two greased and papered layer tins. Mix 1 tablespoonful of cocoa with 1 tablespoonful of boiling water and add to the remainder. Add the raisins, over which a little flour has been sprinkled. Use this for the middle layer. Bake in a hot oven 15 to 20 minutes. Put together and ice with Moca icing.

Cake Icings

Fluffy Icing

1½ c. granulated sugar	1 tsp. vanilla extract
¾ c. water	½ tsp. almond extract
2 egg whites	

Boil sugar and water without stirring until the sirup spins a hair when dropped from spoon. Pour sirup slowly on stiffly beaten egg whites, beating constantly until stiff enough to spread. Add flavorings and mix.

Mocha Icing

1 Tb. butter	3 Tb. strong boiled coffee
1 Tb. cocoa (dry)	1 tsp. vanilla
2 c. confectioner's sugar (rolled)	

Cream butter, add cocoa, sugar, coffee, and vanilla, a little of each at a time, beating constantly until all ingredients are mixed and icing is of right consistency to spread.

Institute Clubs May *Share* Ideas

By KATHERINE RABUCK
Club Secretary

THROUGHOUT this month's INSPIRATION, you are reminded that the Woman's Institute came into being just eight years ago, and you are probably marveling with every one else over the almost unbelievable accomplishments of these years. Since the very beginning, it has been a constant repetition of "something attempted, something done," the Institute having brought to thousands and thousands of women both opportunity for greater accomplishment and the security that comes from confident knowledge. And you who belong to the Woman's Institute Clubs can vouch for the benefit you have received through the development of the club activities.

Knowing how helpful the exchange of ideas among you has been, you can readily see how much your horizon will be extended if this interchange can be effected among Clubs. "And how can this be done?" you ask. We have a plan in mind that, with your cooperation, will be very easy of accomplishment.

AS home women occupied with family or public interests or as business women engaged in the activities of the business world, you may know:

Short-cut methods for tedious processes.

Little economies that can be effected in home management or dress.

Ways to add variety and interest to irksome and monotonous duties, like the preparation of the three daily meals. Little conveniences that will save steps for some busy mother.

How to prepare dishes that call out a chorus of long-drawn "Ohs" and "Ahs" from the children and bring the intimate little glance of appreciation from "the best man in the world."

Some new ideas in home decoration that combine small cost with real beauty.

How to systematize your living in such a way as to give you more leisure for self-improvement and recreation.

How to plan your clothes so that they give you the greatest service and variety.

The secret of successful "make-overs" and therefore how to look well-dressed always.

Ways to add to your income or to provide luxuries that could not otherwise be afforded.

Simple every-day means right at hand that can be used for money-making.

ENERGETIC, active women are doing things every day that would give zest and interest to the work and lives of others if the "finds" could be passed along.

Just such women with just such ideas are to be found in all our Clubs, and many others will be there who will need the "helps" you can give. So, realizing this, I am going to ask you to write brief accounts of the helpful ideas that you have worked out or have found, sign your name and that of the Club to which you belong, and then tuck them into your work basket or hand-bag for your next Club meeting. Read them to your Club members during your discussion period and then let your Club President send them to me so that I, in turn, may pass them on to other Clubs. Sharing our "improvement secrets" in this way, we shall be enriched in the giving.

INTERESTING CLUB NEWS

A CLUB president writes of how much the making of the One Hour dress was enjoyed. One of the members, who was in need of a new home dress, brought blue chambray to the meeting for which this particular work was planned. One member did the cutting, another took measurements, and the rest gathered about with their booklets of directions and followed carefully each step of the work. And the serviceable little dress was completed at the meeting and ready for its blue-eyed wearer to don the next day.

From another Club, we hear that each member came to the meeting one afternoon with material for the Yard-Square apron tucked in her work bag, some of the members making their aprons while the program was under way and all working out original ideas of development. A number of the Club members waited until the talk was over and then had a contest to see who could make the apron in the shortest time and still have her work satisfactory. It was a very interesting meeting and one that was enlivened by much wholesome fun.

Aim at The *Highest*

By SARA L. BYRNE
Assistant Director of Instruction

A FAVORITE expression of one of my school professors was "Aim at the highest—there's always room at the top." It came to me today as I was thinking about our graduates, for they must have had some thought such as this in their minds when they enrolled for their Course of study. But the important point is that they *kept* the thought in mind until they reached the goal for which they started.

For anything worth while that comes to us, we must put forth some effort and perhaps make some sacrifice, but, of course, that just makes us appreciate it all the more. And so, what I want to do today is to urge you to keep before you what you can accomplish through the study of your Course, for then I know you will work for your diploma.

One of our Millinery graduates writes:

"Yes, I was tempted more than once during my Course to give it up, but there was something in me that kept me from it and I've been glad now for that something. The satisfaction that I have now dispels all the doubts I had before."

Another graduate, this one a Dressmaking student, says:

"Did I ever feel like giving up? Oh dear yes, many a time, but I kept saying to myself at those times, 'Don't be a slacker; look ahead and think of the wee folks' and I'd dig in again, determined to win out. And so I have."

One of our Cookery graduates, 18 years of age, and living on a farm in Illinois, says:

"I began my Course with fear and doubt, but that all quickly vanished when I got past the first two lessons. I then became so deeply interested that I was always reluctant to stop. I am truly glad I went on and completed the Course. It has been so much help to me here in our own home, even if I haven't a home of my very own to look after."

THE awarding of a diploma is a real happiness at the Institute. The coming of the final examinations, the ordering of the diploma, the personal signatures, all mean that a graduate is in the making and give occasion for happy pride on the part of all concerned, especially the graduate.

Will you be a graduate in 1924? You, alone, can answer that question. Say that you will, and we will help you in every possible way to carry out your resolution.

The great art of learning is to learn a little at a time, and knowledge is a storehouse of wealth upon which you, as banker, may deposit or draw at your own convenience.

So work for a definite goal. Study a little every day. Be a graduate.

Fashion Service
— SUPPLEMENT —

Each Issue of *Vintage Notions Monthly* includes a *Fashion Service Supplement*. You will read about the fashion styles popular in the early twentieth century and receive a collectible fashion illustration to print and frame.

The students of the Woman's Institute would also receive a publication called *Fashion Service*. Where the *Inspiration* newsletter instructed them on all aspects of the domestic arts, not only sewing but also cooking, housekeeping, decorating, etc., *Fashion Service* was devoted entirely to giving current fashions with a key to their development.

Fashion Service prided itself on providing it's readers with reliable style information and the newest fashion forecasting. The publication wasn't just eye candy. The Institute stressed the importance of studying the fashions to benefit the sewer's understanding of dressmaking. To quote founder Mary Brooks Picken, "Once the principles of design...and of construction… are understood, beautiful garments will result. This publication comes to you as an aid to this desired goal. Read the text of every page and reason out the why of every illustration and description that your comprehension of designing and construction may be enlarged and your appreciation made more acute."

Today, these articles and illustrations give us a historically accurate view of what fashion really meant 100 years ago. Not only can we study these articles for an "of-the-time" style snapshot, but just as their students did, we can also learn to understand the principles of design and increase our sewing skills. In each issue, look for a collectible illustration in the back of the supplement!

WAIST LINES, THOUGH NOT NEW, IMPART YOUTHFULNESS

Above—Heavy navy Canton crêpe with novelty Hercules braid sounds simple, yet when the braid is of varied color—red, tan, rose, blue, green, and yellow—it takes on a chicness quite unakin to the first impression.

Above—Orchid taffeta shot with blue, blue-and-silver lace, and a young girl make a charming picture. The basque effect, the straight 2¼-yard skirt with just one side seam, and then the band of lace stitched at its upper edge only, bespeak both youth and simplicity. One-half of a ¾-yard piece of lace is used for each sleeve, the cut edges of the lace coming under the binding edge of the sleeves.

Left—Flat crêpe in soft sea-green with pearl trimming makes this semitunic, ultra-smart frock. The fulness in the skirt is arranged in an inverted plait at the center front and the apron tunic is stitched in when the waist and skirt are joined together. The pearl trimming is used to make a line of decoration the full length of the dress and around the waist. Black satin is effective when developed in this simple way with braid and fringe used in place of the pearl banding and ornament.

Left—A becoming dress of figured silk is always desirable, particularly when, like the model shown, it has both grace and charm to recommend it. With 3 yards of 40-inch silk, 2½ yards of velvet-ribbon, a lace collar, and an hour's time, this dress may be made and worn with pleasure.

YOUTH, DIGNITY, AND SIMPLICITY, ALL POSSIBLE IN THE NEW

Velvet, Moiré, and Crêpe are Favorites for Party and Dance Frocks

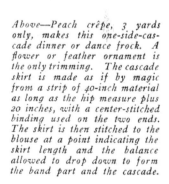

Above—Delicate flesh moiré, silver lace, and a feather flower of blue combine to make this demure frock suitable for dancing or evening wear. A 2-yard piece of 40-inch moiré is used crosswise for the skirt, the hem being made on one selvage and the wide tuck on the fold of the material. A straight piece of silver lace, 1¼ yards long, is frilled in slightly at the neck to give a bertha effect, and the ends are left open at the center back, where a long blue-velvet streamer covers the ends.

Above—Peach crêpe, 3 yards only, makes this one-side-cascade dinner or dance frock. A flower or feather ornament is the only trimming. The cascade skirt is made as if by magic from a strip of 40-inch material as long as the hip measure plus 20 inches, with a center-stitched binding used on the two ends. The skirt is then stitched to the blouse at a point indicating the skirt length and the balance allowed to drop down to form the band part and the cascade.

Left—One hour's time, 2 yards of erect-pile velvet in brown, with ½ yard of metallic cloth in a harmonizing color, and 6½ yards of brown moiré ribbon, will make a dress as smart and lovely as this. The metallic cloth is split crosswise and the skirt is made just as wide as the two strips when seamed together. Plaited ribbon covers the seam that joins the metallic cloth and the velvet. The ribbon at the neck is stitched straight across the front for a distance of 6 or 7 inches and the ends are brought back and knotted at the waist line in the back, with streamers hanging below the knee bend.

YOUTHFUL TYPES ARE SMARTLY CLOTHED

Normal Waist Lines, Flares, and
Basques Belong to Lithesome Youth

Model 8.—The tunic-blouse section of this dress is cut in one piece by following the instruction for the Straight-Line, One-Piece Dress. Slant the under-arm seam out very slightly toward the selvages instead of cutting straight in from the edge at the hip line. It is not necessary to add a great amount of width through the hips for the three slits from the bottom of the tunic up to the hip line give ease. The skirt is merely a straight piece of the material attached to the tunic at the hip line with a single seam. Shape the back of the neck slightly, but in the front merely slash it down far enough to allow it to be slipped over the head. Turn back the corners thus made for lapels, facing them with self-material. A slit on the fold of each lapel near the point permits of bringing the tie through in the novel manner illustrated.

Model 8A.—Follow the instruction for the Straight-Line, One-Piece Dress in cutting this frock. Since this model has no side plaits, cut on down from the point indicated by *i* in Fig. 4, Page 10, to the bottom of the material, slanting the line of cutting only very slightly toward the selvage. In case the lower edge of the skirt is not quite even, lift up the sides by taking a small horizontal dart over each hip at the normal waist line where it will be covered by the belt. Face the front-opening slash invisibly. The only fastening is accomplished by means of the link buttons at the top of the slash. Take great care to place the square patch pockets at the most becoming point, and stitch them very accurately close to the edge.

Model 8B.—For cutting the type of dress which has closely fitted shoulder lines and set-in sleeves, a well-fitting pattern is quite essential. Pictorial Review pattern 2420 may be adapted to this model. Simply leave the side seams open from a point a few inches below the hip line to the bottom of the tunic and finish the edges by facing them invisibly. The tunic is then worn over a costume slip having a deep band of plaid taffeta at the bottom. The narrow bias band of taffeta, which outlines the waistcoat line, is applied with slip-stitches. At the side openings, one may work real tailored buttonholes or add imitations of braid.

Model 8C.—For the average figure, use 2 or 2¼ yards of Georgette for the tunic-blouse section of this model. Fold it crosswise through the center and then follow the instruction for cutting the Straight-Line, One-Piece Dress, substituting *cut edges* for *selvages*. When the cutting is completed according to directions, slash the material 2 or 2½ inches from *i* in Fig. 4, Page 10, toward

the center fold, cutting through the four thicknesses of the material. The hip fulness is gathered instead of plaited, and the slashes made are for the purpose of giving a seam line for joining the gathered sections. The narrow tie-belts over the hips conceal the joining seams. When the marabou is added to the edge of the tunic, it is distended to give the slightly circular effect shown.

The tunic is worn over a costume slip of the same Georgette. The top of the slip hem should come under the band of marabou so as to be concealed and expose a double thickness of the Georgette in all parts of the dress. A scarf of tulle softens the effect of the whole and puts it in the evening-dress class.

Model 8D.—Follow the Simplicity Two-Piece Dress plan, Page 36, for cutting this quaint little basque model, but make the sleeves as directed for the One-Piece Dress. The hem of the skirt is deep enough to meet the lower edge of the band of the reverse side of the material, which is merely cut out, turned over, and joined again with plain seams. Stitch very accurately in joining these seams, and finish the seam edges by overcasting them. Hunt out a bit of cretonne or chintz of good design with rich coloring—not too bright. Cut out small motifs and appliqué them with chain-stitches, using fine gold thread. This is one of the newest trimming touches.

Collar and cuffs of fine lace may be purchased or made to suit the design. A tiny ribbon bow serves to carry the loveliest color of the appliqué up to the throat.

Model 8E.—For cutting the blouse of this model, fold the 54-inch wool material as directed for the Straight-Line, One-Piece Dress. The lower edge of the blouse will be cut as a continuation of the line that cuts straight in from the selvage to point *i* in Fig. 4. In cutting the lower edge of the blouse, however, curve it as directed for curving the lower edge of the blouse of the Simplicity Two-Piece Dress. The Two-Piece plan is not used for cutting the whole blouse of this dress because the neck line fits up closely and hence requires shaping on the shoulders. The skirt is made by the Two-Piece plan, all of the fulness being put into one plait that turns toward the front on the left side. This plait conceals the one seam of the skirt. The knee-depth tuck, which gives the effect of a deep tunic blouse, is stitched before the side seam is made.

If a cloth belt is used across the front, its ends may be joined to the dress in the side seams. But if a leather belt is used, small openings may be provided in the side seams of the blouse, and the belt run through them so that it is exposed in the front only.

YOUTH CHOOSES DISCRIMINATELY

Model 8

8 A

8 B

8 C

8 D

8 E

A satisfying sight, indeed, is a young girl of chestnut type in a soft flannel dress of burnt russet. The straight skirt of Model 8 is slipped under the tunic and joined with a row of stitching. Black tie and cuffs, and tiny silver buttons and buckles give accent to this costume.

A collar of creamy tan matches in color the suède belt that defines the normal waist line of Model 8A. Strawberry flannel is the material and the only trimming is the novelty banding that edges the sleeves and patch pockets.

The three-quarter-length navy serge tunic of Model 8B is left open to the hips on the side seams. Plaid taffeta adds a pleasing color touch. An applied bias band of the taffeta gives the waistcoat effect.

Gray fur or self-colored marabou banding gives body to the tunic of the turquoise-blue Georgette party dress shown in Model 8C. The simple kimono-sleeve tunic, which is cut with a circular flare at the hips, is worn over a Georgette slip.

The black crêpe satin of Model 8D is brightened by cut-out chintz flowers, which are applied with chain-stitches of gold metallic thread. The band in the skirt, which shows the reverse side of the material, is joined with plain seams.

The skirt of Model 8E is tucked to simulate a tunic. A deep plait turns toward the front on the left side. The lengthwise grain of the material is used across the figure for the skirt. A red collar and front belt and embroidered banding add color.

UNLIMITED VARIETY IN BLOUSES AND SKIRTS

Tunics and Overblouses for Many Occasions, and
Skirts That Are Simple, Serviceable, and Smart

Model 9.—Follow the plan for cutting the Straight-Line, One-Piece Dress, Page 10, making the changes suggested below. The embroidery may be done in running-stitches or couching, or beads may be used, if preferred. The neck, sleeves, and lower edge of the blouse are finished with narrow facings blind-stitched on the wrong side. A finish that would show on the right side would compete with the design of the embroidery and detract from its appearance.

Model 9A.—By using the crosswise grain of bengaline up and down, this blouse may be cut by the Straight-Line, One-Piece Dress plan. It is not necessary to add much to the width of this blouse through the hips, for the four slits from the bottom up to the hip line take care of that very nicely. Make from four to six straight slits in the sleeves at their lower edges and bind these with bias binding. Gather them into straight bands, which are close-fitting and are finished by snapping the ends together. Arrange an opening on the left shoulder.

Model 9B.—Use the lengthwise grain of the material across the figure and cut the blouse by the Straight-Line, One-Piece Dress plan. Sew up the under-arm seams from the sleeve to the low waist line. Leave them open below that, finishing them with a narrow blind-stitched facing and fastening the blouse by means of buttons and loops. Finish the edges of the scarf with picoting, and join it to the neck line at the left-side front in the seam that holds the neck facing. The cuffs are merely double bands applied straight.

Model 9C.—Cut this model by the Straight-Line, One-Piece Dress plan, cutting entirely across the material on the hip line that cuts in straight to the under-arm seam. Use the lengthwise grain of the material around the figure. Do not shape the neck line in the front. Merely slash the center-front fold down as far as the opening is desired and shape the back-neck line. Cut a facing for the front, having it wide enough to extend out about 1 inch onto each shaped shoulder line, and 2 inches deeper than the front slit. Put it right side down over the right side of the blouse front. Stitch around the opening slit, close to the

edge. Turn the facing to the wrong side and press it. The band of pin tucking is then applied to the edge. This, as well as the bands on the sleeves, must be lined with a band of the plain crêpe. Mark the position for the front inserts and cut out a piece of the material on each side, allowing for plain seams for joining the inserts.

Model 9D.—Use the lengthwise grain of the material around the figure and cut by the Straight-Line, One-Piece Dress plan. If crêpe satin is used, bands of the dull side of the material may be applied for trimming, keeping the stitching very close to the edges of the band. If preferred, a light-weight wool material may be used as a trimming on a silk blouse, and the whole worn with a wool skirt or shammed slip to match.

Model 9E.—Cut this blouse by the Straight-Line, One-Piece Dress plan, but cut the back section longer than the front to allow for the tucks that occur below the waist line. Leave the under-arm seams open below the waist line, and finish them with blind-stitched facings. If embroidery banding is used to decorate the front, it may be applied over the crêpe, but if lace is used, cut the material away underneath it.

Model 9F.—Knife plait the lower charmeuse section of this slip and attach it to a slip top that is cut and fitted as described for Model 14. This top may be of lighter-weight material, such as crêpe de Chine.

Model 9G.—This is a straight one-piece skirt, made from a single width of 54-inch material. For a larger figure, it is necessary to use the lengthwise grain of the material around the figure. Have it fit slightly loose around the hips and gather the small amount of fulness so that it falls over the hips and in the back. The left-side front trimming is merely an applied band of the material covering the one seam and the placket.

Model 9H.—If a perfectly straight one-piece skirt does not give enough width at the lower edge for comfort, arrange an inverted plait at the left-side front. A habit-back placket is concealed in this plait. The lengthwise grain of the material may be used around the figure.

METHOD OF CUTTING THE BLOUSES

The blouses that are shown on Page 29 may be cut by the Straight-Line, One-Piece Dress plan. Since silk materials rarely exceed 40 inches in width, it is necessary to use the crosswise grain of the material up and down. For the average figure, 1½ yards makes the body part of even the longest blouse shown. More material must be supplied for sleeves, of course. Follow the instructions given on **Page 10** for cutting the dress, substituting the words *cut edges* for *selvages,* and make the first fold through the center *crosswise* rather than *lengthwise.* In cutting, slant the under-arm seam out very slightly toward the cut edges instead of cutting straight in from the edge at the hip line, as directed for the dress.

BLOUSES ARE LONG AND SKIRTS CHIC

Simple running-stitch embroidery or beading and metal buttons form the center of attraction of Model 9. The material is russet crêpe de Chine.

Navy bengaline fashions a tunic blouse that may become a part of a costume. The sleeve treatment of Model 9A is unusual. The collar is of organdie.

Inverted side plaits give necessary width to Model 9B, a tunic blouse of chenille chiffon, with attached scarf of plain chiffon in a harmonizing color.

Pin tucks prove their decorative value in the development of Model 9C from modest gray crêpe de Chine. The narrow red tie adds a pleasing color touch.

Wood-brown crêpe satin is employed in Model 9D. The crêpe side of the material is used in conjunction with novelty buttons for trimming.

Red embroidery bands brighten the dark-blue flat crêpe of which Model 9E is made, while the pin tucks in the back relieve its plainness.

A change of costume need not mean complete disrobing. A costume slip like Model 9F of black charmeuse may be worn under many tunic blouses of various types in as rapid succession as you wish.

A flannel sports skirt checked in shades of tan, as shown in Model 9G, is an outstanding success from any viewpoint. A stitched-on band of the material covers the seam.

Comfort sacrifices nothing to smartness in the russet kasha skirt shown in Model 9H. The inverted plait has numerous reasons for being.

The plaited apron of Model 10 gives its wearer credit for every one of her thirteen years, without the least suggestion of a too early sophistication. Developed of Flemish-blue crêpe de Chine, it is logically collared and cuffed with guipure lace.

Even a chubby child looks nearly as slim, and fully as sweet, as the stick of candy that her striped-flannel dress resembles if it is made of the material shown in Model 10A. Plain flannel makes the collar, cuffs, and belt.

The long-wearing quality of blue serge becomes a virtue, even to Miss Ten-Year-Old, when it means prolonging for an indefinite time the joy of possessing a dress like Model 10B, with its silk-braid trimming and its tiny silvery buttons.

Girlish dignity is delightfully expressed by Model 10E. Blue serge is the material. Cuffs and vest are of plaited crêpe de Chine in red, rust, or green, to suit the wearer's coloring and youthful fancy. The leather belt matches the vest in color.

In a season when plaids are so beautiful, what school girl would not find joy in the wearing of a simple little affair like Model 10D, with its long scarf collar and belt of plain flannel of the plaid's predominant color? The buttons that outline the front closing are of the color of the plain flannel.

A cozy dress for a little girl's school hours is made of flannel in collie color, a soft tan, after the manner of Model 10C. For trimming, it has bright wool blanket-stitching on the front opening, and groups of tiny brass buttons.

For her party frock, crisp peach-colored taffeta, of course! Rows of ribbon, with outstanding loops, distend the hips of the applied Georgette panels of Model 10F with pannier-like bouffancy. A vest of cream Georgette and bows of the same ribbon further decorate the dress. If she prefers, the whole dress may be of the taffeta.

WHAT THE WELL-DRESSED JUNIOR WEARS

Whether for School or Parties, Her Costume is Suited to the Occasion

Model 10.—Cut and make this dress by the Straight-Line, One-Piece Dress plan, Page 10. For each of the tiers of the plaited apron, supply a strip of material three times as long as the finished width of the apron from side to side. Attach the lower tier to a straight sham-piece that is 1 inch shorter and ½ inch narrower than the upper tier when it lies flat after plaiting. Pin the upper tier over the sham and join both together in a belt with long ends for ties. Attach the completed apron to the dress with snap fasteners under the belt.

Model 10A.—The Straight-Line, One-Piece Dress plan is used again when it comes to cutting this slenderizing dress for a chubby little girl. Do not shape the front of the neck line as described in the cutting directions on Page 10. Instead, merely slit the front down as far as it is desired to have the opening extend. Shape the back of the neck, however. Cut a facing section for the lapel-like part of the collar, having it wide enough from side to side to extend out about 1 inch over each shaped shoulder line, and 2 inches deeper than the center-front slit. In applying the facing, put it on the right side of the dress with its right side down, and stitch around the slit opening very close to the edge. Turn the facing to the wrong side and press it.

Then apply the scarf collar, which is a straight piece of plain flannel of the color predominant in the striped material. It is double and applied to the neck edge in much the same way that a bias binding is applied to an edge. A bit of wool fringe finishes the long end.

Model 10B.—This model is not nearly so complicated as it appears, for it is cut by the Straight-Line, One-Piece Dress plan. The lines that give it its distinction are formed by the application of narrow military braid. The joining of the tiny vest is concealed and its line outlined by a band of braid. Tiny buttons finish off the ends of the braid on the left side and effect the center-front closing.

Model 10C.—The little middy-like blouse of this model is cut like the upper part of the Straight-Line, One-Piece Dress. It stops at the hip line, however, where it is cut across. The skirt is a plain little wrap-around model, cut in one straight piece, overlapped from 4 to 8 inches at the side front, and attached to a little under-waist or camisole. The buttons on the skirt are sewed through both thicknesses, thus holding them together. Cut a rather deep front opening in the blouse and finish the edges with blanket-stitching in wool.

Model 10D.—In cutting this dress by the Straight-Line, One-Piece Dress plan, an allowance of 2 inches must be made for the overlapping of the full-length front opening. This may be provided as follows:

Make a 3-inch turn toward the wrong side on each selvage. These will provide the front facings and linings of the lapels. Overlap these edges as they will be in the finished dress and pin them securely. The material is now in the form of a tube. When it is laid flat on the table, there will be a fold on each edge. Have the fold nearest to you at the point planned for the center front of the dress. Then fold the material in half lengthwise, turning the center-front fold up, or away from you, when it will be in the position shown in Fig. 4, Page 10, except that there will be two folds where the selvages are shown. In cutting, slant the under-arm seam out slightly toward these folds. Attach the collar as directed for Model 10A.

Model 10E.—Follow the Straight-Line, One-Piece Dress plan in cutting this dress, but shape the deep U-shaped neck in front, as shown. Sew a 1½-inch binding to the wrong side of the plaiting with a ¼-inch seam, as at *a* in the figure below. Crease the binding away from this stitching and baste it to the skirt, as at *b*. Turn the free edge of the binding over ⅜ inch, as at *c*. Turn this edge over the stitching line *a* and stitch through the center, as at *d*. This stitching also joins the plaiting to the skirt.

Model 10F.—Cut and make the foundation dress of taffeta by the Straight-Line, One-Piece Dress plan. Cut the Georgette side sections straight and apply the ribbon to them. Then gather the tops and apply these sections with a center-stitched Georgette binding. Also use this binding for the neck and sleeves.

The figure at the left illustrates the method of applying the plaited flounce described under Model 10E.

CHANGES IN CUTTING FOR CHILDREN

To cut dresses for children by either the Straight-Line, One-Piece, or the Simplicity Two-Piece plan, take the measurements in the same way as you would for an adult. The only change that is necessary is to cut the neck line higher. This plan will necessitate the cutting of a 4-inch opening, which can be arranged to come in the center back, the center front, or on the shoulder, depending on the design of the particular dress you are planning to make.

JUVENILES BORROW GROWN-UP STYLE EFFECTS

The Simplicity of Line of Popular Styles Makes
Them Readily Adaptable to Children's Wear

Model 11.—For the tucked inserts, collar, and cuffs of this model, cut strips of green taffeta slightly wider than the finished sections are to be, and allow several inches additional in length. Do the tucking with the tucker, first setting it for $\frac{1}{16}$-inch tucks, 1 inch apart. A further saving of time is possible by using the binder in applying the black military braid. To turn a square corner, bind one edge until about $\frac{1}{8}$ inch from the corner. Stop the machine with the needle in the material, raise the presser bar, place a stiletto in the scroll of the binder and turn the material squarely around in position to bind the other edge. Push up enough binding on the under side to allow for turning the corner. Finish the wrong side by hand. If a pattern is desired for this model, use Pictorial Review pattern 2426.

Model 11A.—Follow the Simplicity Two-Piece Dress plan, Page 36, for this dress. The skirt fulness is confined in one inverted plait on the left-side front. The band of plain flannel that ends in a point over the inverted plait is stitched flat to the blouse after having its edges turned under. A short, bound-slit opening in the center front gives ample room for the dress to slip over the head, and is concealed by the tie.

Model 11B.—For this dressy coat, use McCall pattern 3786. Size 8 requires $1\frac{7}{8}$ yards of 48-inch material without nap, or $1\frac{3}{4}$ yards of 54-inch material with nap. For the lining, provide $2\frac{1}{4}$ yards of 36-inch material. Beaver-fur banding makes the collar and cuffs, $1\frac{1}{4}$ yards being the amount required.

Model 11C.—This very dignified little coat with its scarf collar may be cut after Excella pattern E1690. An eight-year-old girl will require approximately $1\frac{3}{4}$ yards of 54-inch broadcloth, $1\frac{7}{8}$ yards of 36-inch material for lining, and $1\frac{1}{8}$ yards of narrow squirrel banding.

Model 11D.—Cut the foundation dress by the Straight-Line, One-Piece plan, Page 10. To this shirr the bias apron front, the edges of which are finished with the center-stitched binding. Attach the bias neck frill with the same stitching that holds the center-stitched binding. Join the tops of the bias puff sleeves with plain seams, and finish their lower edges with bias bands applied to resemble the center-stitched binding, as shown below.

Model 11E.—This little Straight-Line, One-Piece Dress has a section removed in the front of the skirt, and a black-satin plaited section inserted. Allow for plain seams both on the dress and on the inserted section. An opening may be arranged under the front embroidery.

Model 11F.—Choose a plain little kimono-sleeve pattern, such as McCall 3484, for cutting this dress. Decide on the number of scallops desired and divide the width of the bottom of the pattern into as many equal parts. Outline the lower edge of the scallops, and $\frac{1}{2}$ inch on each side of the point where two scallops join draw a straight line up as far as it is desired to have the insert extend. Cut the pattern and apply the binding and puffing as the illustration below indicates.

Model 11G.—A pattern which duplicates this model is Pictorial Review pattern 2434. The four-year-old size requires approximately 1 yard each of 36-inch material for the blouse and the trousers. A straight band of material like the trousers is stitched in V-shape to conceal the joining of the vest and blouse.

Model 11H.—Any plain trousers pattern may be used for cutting this model by outlining the pointed extensions on a piece of paper pinned to the top of the pattern. Use a plain blouse pattern having a center-front plait, and apply tiny frills to each side of it.

When the braid for making the motifs for Model 11B has been folded and straightened out, it will appear as in view (a). Make three diagonal folds, as at a, b, and c, view (b), bringing the long end toward you in each case, and always folding at right angles. When these folds are completed, slip the long end d under the short one e, cut them even length, and turn both to the wrong side so that the finished motif appears as in view c. Tack the ends invisibly.

Gather the bottom of the sleeve of Model 11D. Cut bias strips 1½ inches wide and apply as a center-stitched binding with a ¼-inch seam, as at a, a ⅜-inch turn, as at b, and a center stitching, as at c.

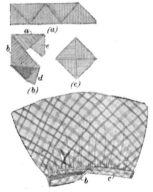

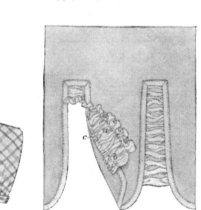

To make the attractive finish for the bottom of the skirt of Model 11F, first bind the scallops, using the binding attachment. See the directions for turning corners given under Model 11. Do not stretch the material in binding the curves, and do not feed it in too fast. Cut the puffed inserts 1 inch wider than the space between the scallops. Gather each side ½ inch from the edge, as at a, using the ruffler. Slip-stitch the puffing to the edges of the scallops, having the gathering threads come near the outer edge of the binding, as at b. Turn under the raw edge of the puffing ¼ inch and whip it to the other edge of the binding, as at c.

STYLES FOR THE ACTIVE AGE

Tucked green taffeta for collar, cuffs, and insert brightens a blue-serge school dress with bindings of black silk braid in Model 11.

Plaid flannel or taffeta forms the blouse, and plain harmonizing flannel, the skirt and applied band of Model 11A. The white collar is washable.

A soft suède-finished material in shutter green makes the cunning coat shown as Model 11B. Silk braid motifs ornament the sleeves and cape. Beaver fur is used for the collar and cuffs.

The material of Model 11C is broadcloth, the color, burnt russet, and the trimming, squirrel fur.

A shirred-on apron front of bias self-material is an arresting feature of Model 11D, which is developed in plaid taffeta. Tiny puff sleeves are quaint and cunning.

The strawberry wool crêpe dress, Model 11E, introduces front fulness in a plaited insert of black satin. The embroidery banding is mostly black.

Shirred inserts of pink Georgette and embroidered pink rosebuds add a French touch to a pale-blue taffeta party dress, such as Model 11F. A yellow dress with white inserts gives the needed dash for a brunette child.

A two-piece washable suit, made like Model 11G, has trousers of coffee-brown linen buttoned to a white linen or cotton blouse with brown linen trimmings.

A dressier suit is shown in Model 11H. The trousers are of blue serge and the blouse, of plain white wash silk or soisette. Brown rep and natural pongee may be substituted, if preferred.

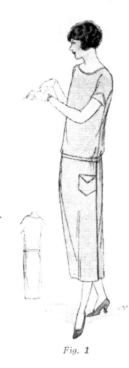

Fig. 1

The type of two-piece dress shown in Fig. 1, when attractively made of smart new material, is a joy to own. It is adaptable to a variety of fabrics, from wool to calico, from Swiss to chiffon; in fact, any fabric that does not have a definite nap, such as flat-pile velvet, broadcloth, or similar materials, can be used. Stripes are very good for it, used lengthwise in the blouse and around in the skirt.

Measurements and Width of Materials.—Take the measurements exactly the same as for the one-piece dress on Page 10.

If you are more than a 38-inch bust, use 40-inch material. If you are less than 38, 36-inch material is satisfactory. And if you are less than 34, 32-inch material may be used. From 3 to 3½ yards of 36- or 40-inch material is required.

If you are tall and slender, the only waste in cutting the dress will be that cut out in shaping the neck.

Dividing the Material.—You now divide your material into two parts, one for the blouse and one for the skirt, as in Fig. 2.

Measure off from one end the *blouse length,* and place a pin in the edge of the material to mark the point. Clip through the selvage and cut or tear across.

Cutting the Armhole and Under Arm.—Fold the shorter piece of material, or the blouse length, first lengthwise, selvage edges together, and then crosswise, as in Fig. 3. Bring one crosswise end up 1 inch to make the front longer than the back and allow for fulness over the bust. Measure to the left from the crosswise fold *a* along the selvage one-half the armhole measure and place a pin, as at *b*. Measure from the fold *c* one-fourth the hip measure plus 1½ inches and place a pin, as at *d*.

To obtain the armhole curve, measure straight to the right of *d* 8 or 10 inches and place a pin, as at *e*. Next, cut straight in from *b*, turning as the pin at *e* is approached and making a smooth, even curve. Then cut straight down from *e* to *d*, as shown by the dotted line.

Shaping the Waist Line and Sleeves.—To shape the waist line of the blouse, measure up from the bottom ½ to ⅝ inch and place a pin, as at *f*. On the upper piece, which is for the back, taper a curved line from *f* to a point

Fig. 2

half-way between the under arm and the lengthwise fold. For the front, cut in a curved line on the lower piece from *f* toward *c* to a point slightly more than half way, as shown.

If a pointed sleeve is desired, measure up 3½ inches from *b* on the sleeve line and then cut in a diagonal line from *a* to the 3½-inch point.

Cutting Out the Neck.—Now, to cut the neck, as in Fig. 4, open out the blouse on the crosswise fold and turn it so that the folded edge is toward you and the back or short part of the blouse comes to your left. Measure up on the crosswise crease 4½ inches and mark with a pin, as at *a*. Measure 1 inch on the back fold from the crosswise crease and mark with a pin, as at *b*. Measure to the right from the crosswise crease 4½ inches and mark with a pin, as at *c*.

Cut the front-neck curve by cutting from *c* to *a* and the back curve by cutting from *b* to *a*.

Utilizing the Under-Arm Sections.—When the blouse is cut, it should appear as in Fig. 5, which shows also the sections cut out at the under arms. Use one of these sections for cutting 1½-inch bias binding for finishing the neck, the bottom of the sleeves, and the pockets, and the other for 6- by 9-inch pockets, as shown. Shape the points of the pockets if the sleeves have been shaped, but if they are straight, cut the pockets the same size but with a straight turn-over at the top.

Proportioning the Skirt.—You now cut the belt and skirt from the larger piece of material, as in Fig. 6. For the belt, measure 2½ inches from one selvage edge and cut a strip the full length of the material, cutting on a lengthwise thread. Measure the skirt length from the cut edge down toward the selvage. The material that remains may be used for a hem.

The skirt material should be wide enough to provide for the hip measure plus 6 inches for ease and 20 inches for plaits, each of the two large plaits taking up 8 inches, or 16 inches for both, and each of the four small plaits 1 inch, or 4 inches in all. Thus, if your hip measure is 40 inches, you will need 40 + 26, or 66 inches.

Binding the Neck.—Seam the binding strips to make a center-stitched binding for the neck. To do this, join two or three bias pieces by

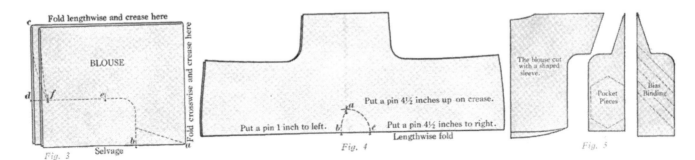

Fig. 3   *Fig. 4*   *Fig. 5*

placing the lengthwise ends together, stitching in a ¼-inch seam, and pressing open with the fingers.

Place the right side of the binding to the wrong side of the neck and stitch in a ¼-inch seam. Begin stitching at one shoulder and stitch across the back of the neck and around toward the front. Do this without stretching either the neck or the binding. Stitch all the way around and join the binding in a bias seam where it meets.

Crease the binding on the under side up from the stitching line *a*, Fig. 7. Then turn the free edge of the binding over ⅜ inch, as at *b*, drawing the edge up smooth and even and creasing as straight as possible. Turn the creased edge *b* down well over the stitching line *a*, and stitch through the center, as at *c*. Begin the stitching at the shoulder and proceed around the back as before.

Finishing the Sleeves.—To bind the two sleeves, join three strips of the binding, open the seams, place the right side of the binding to the right side of the sleeve, as at *a*, Fig. 8, and stitch in a ¼-inch seam. Turn the binding to the wrong side and make a center-stitched binding. Turn back in cuff effect, as shown at *b*.

When the material is attractive on the wrong side, a center-stitched binding may be made from the sleeve itself as a cuff finish without using a binding piece. To make this, first turn up ⅜ to ½ inch and then make another ½-inch turn. Stitch directly in the center. This will give the same effect as the binding used at the neck.

When this finish is applied, as in a cuff or a cascade, turn the edges in at the corner in square effect before stitching.

Completing the Blouse.—With the sleeve finish completed, sew the under-arm seams, wrong sides together, for a French seam. Turn and complete the seams. At the bottom of the sleeves, turn and stitch back in the stitching line just made about 1 inch to secure the cuff edge and to stay the thread ends.

Hemming and Seaming the Skirt.—If a plain hem is to be used, the skirt will have to be seamed first, a French seam being used in sheer materials and a plain seam with group overcasting, Fig. 9, in heavy materials. A plain

hem may be turned and machine-stitched in, or it may be slip-stitched, as in Fig. 10. Before slip-stitching a hem, first turn the top of the hem edge down ¼ inch, as at *a*, and stitch by machine. This gives a firm edge that will aid in keeping a straight line and also protect the slip-stitches. To slip-stitch easily, hold the skirt side next to you, as at *b*, having the fingers on the hem side. Take up as little material with each stitch as possible. To avoid pulling or puckering the hemming-stitches, hold the hem secure and take a back-stitch every 6 or 7 stitches, as at *c*.

Another simple finish is the cuff hem shown in Fig. 11. This should be put in before the skirt seam is stitched.

To make a cuff hem, turn the hem portion to the right side, creasing on a lengthwise thread. Turn the edge over ⅜ inch and turn the fold ½ inch. Press down and stitch directly in the center.

If a cuff hem is used, prepare to French seam the skirt, as in Fig. 11. Pin the bottom *a* and top *b* of the hem ends together so that they will be perfectly even and cannot slip during the stitching.

Contrary to the regular rule, begin the stitching of the skirt at the bottom. Stay the end of the seam by beginning 1 inch from the bottom, as at *c*, stitching to the bottom, and then turning and stitching the full length of the seam. Turn wrong side out and complete the French seam, remembering to stay each end.

If you desire, the hem may be omitted and binding or braid used to finish the bottom of the skirt.

Putting in the Skirt Plaits.—Lay a 4-inch plait on one side of the skirt, having the seam come at the inside of the plait, as shown in Fig. 12. This plait may be laid toward the back or the front, and should be pressed in straight.

About 1½ inches each side of this plait, lay a small plait, about ½ inch deep, as shown, to take up all extra fulness. As both sides are alike, measure half way around the skirt and pin three similar plaits in the opposite side. The edges of each deep plait should come at the under-arm seam of the waist.

If the figure is full across the back in the hips, an inverted plait, with each plait made 2 inches deep and the edges turned to meet, is more satisfactory than the deep 4-inch plait.

Continued on page 30

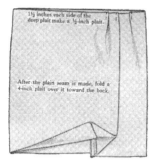

Fig. 12

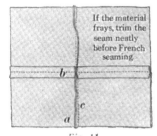

If the material frays, trim the seam neatly before French seaming.

Fig. 11

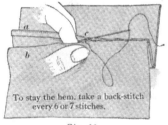

To stay the hem, take a back-stitch every 6 or 7 stitches.

Fig. 10

Fig. 9

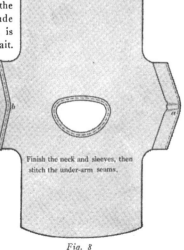

Finish the neck and sleeves, then stitch the under-arm seams.

Fig. 6

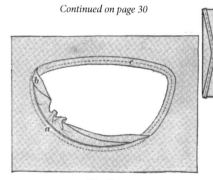

Fig. 7

Fig. 8

12 A

12 B

Model 12

12 C

12 D

12 E

FABRICS OF PRIME IMPORTANCE

*F*ABRIC for making and trimming is a style point this season, possessing many possibilities for unique effects. This idea is very pronounced in the group of smart street hats illustrated on this page. A navy felt skirt makes the entire hat and high out-shooting loop in Model 12. A touch of color is introduced by pasting gray suède or any other contrasting color under the cut-out designs in the felt around the brim and on the loop that serves as a trim.

Although newer shapes are seeking recognition, the frameless "crusher," with its flared-up left side and front, which shapes down into a long point at the right side, as shown in Model 12A, retains favor. This model is developed in lacquer-red velvet with motifs of black felt appliquéd on the brim and crown tip, making an all-over pattern design that is most pleasing. Hats of this type, carried out in autumn color scheme, are smart adjuncts to the new polo coats.

A combination of fabric, brown Lyons velvet and teakwood suède, is used for Model 12B, the broad-brimmed hat with drooping sides and slightly rolling back. The under facing, the upper-edge flange, and the divisions between the crown sections are of velvet. The inner-top facing and four crown sections of suède are French finished to the velvet. A fold of the same velvet around the base of the crown and a tiny bow at the right side complete this model. Additional decoration and coloring may be appropriately applied by the introduction of hand-painted flower sprays on the suède section of the crown.

Demurely drooped, a fit frame for the soft features of youth, is the medium-sized poke in Model 12C. Burnt-russet panne velvet is used to cover the brim and high telescope crown. Extending beyond the brim edge and part way up on the side crown is a sparse ruche of tan faille ribbon. Encircling the crown base is a band of fur, finished at the right side with a metallic flower.

The latest and, at the moment, smartest version of the Spanish sailor is shown in Model 12D. This large, rolling brim is constructed of black Lyons velvet. Its severely plain, high, square crown of black panne has a band of flat bluebirds nested around its base as the only ornamentation.

Among the characteristic fall shapes, the broad, rolled front in Model 12E occupies an important position. Slashed at the right-side front, the brim of this model is covered with black Lyons velvet. The tip of the bowl crown is of black-and-white plaid velvet, while the side piece is black, as is also the glycerined fancy attached at the right-side front. The irregularity of brim line and the combination of materials featured in this model are almost uniformly endorsed by the best designers.

12 F

12 G

12 H

12 I

12 J

DISTINCTIVE HAT MODES

*T*HE quaint little tricorn in Model 12F shows the use of tiny button flowers in capucine tones, appliquéd flat for a facing and a collar effect around the top of the side crown. Bengaline makes the top brim and crown, the rolled ridge through the center front from back to front being pin-tucked and the sides applied plain. The attractiveness of this model lies in its trimness of line and in the warmness of its coloring.

Metallic cloth swirled over a close-fitting visor turban finds new devotees each season. Model 12G differs from last season's model in the long, slender pasted bird that winds itself between the folds of the metallic cloth. The effect of the dull-finished feathers against the shiny fabric of ombrè coloring is very appealing.

Slashed brims have become a most important feature of the season. In Model 12H, the slashed portion of this large, flaring brim continues into the crown on the right side. Black panne velvet is used for the entire top and Lyons for the underfacing. A cord of Venetian fuchsia, the new red violet, is used around the brim edge. A two-toned ostrich blade in the same coloring spreads across the back and off the trim at the right side.

Not only are ribbons employed as trimming, but they frequently form the entire hat, as is the case in Model 12I. Pheasant-colored, fluted ribbon makes this tiny rolled brim and high, square crown of Directoire inspiration. This type of crown is known as the modified postilion because of its slight departure from the conventional shape and the softening of the severity of its crown line by the method used in applying the ribbon. A torsade of dark brown velvet finishes the crown base and a self-colored ostrich brush extends out on the right side.

The smartest tendencies of the season are embodied in Model 12J, with its high, square crown and broad, capeline brim of shutter-green velvet. This shade of green, which is typically American, has soft-grayed tonalities that are restful and inviting. Also, it is a green that all women can wear, as it has none of the harsh tendencies that many members of the green range possess. A crown band of green faille ribbon is topped by a wider one of silver galloon, over which variegated silver rat-tail braid is looped and couched on with green floss.

None of the fall hats are lovelier than the broad-brimmed hat shown in Model 12K and developed in a combination of fabrics. The top brim is of metal brocade and the under facing and loose-edge flange are of sapphire-blue velvet. The top portion of the crown is balloon-shaped, smooth on the tip and then laid in even folds to within 2 inches from the base. This portion is plain with a scroll of metal tubing. Draped softly around the base and tied in a loose bow as a trim, is a bias fold of black velvet.

DEVELOPING THE NEW FALL HATS

Out of the soft velvets, rich brocades, metal cloth, printed duvetyns, deep-ribbed bengaline, and suède that are offered for developing this season's hats, there should be no trouble to select a fabric that is becoming to the wearer and suitable for her needs. The next thought is to determine just how much material is required for making so as not to have any waste, and still avoid a shortage of even an inch, for lack of this amount will ruin the entire effect of the hat.

On flat and slightly drooping brims, the fabric is applied smooth without a seam; that is, the fulness may be drawn and pinned out.

In the case of rolled brims and irregular shapes, where it is impossible to fit the fulness out, the material is shaped around to conform to the brim and the fulness worked to one point, a joining or a seam being then used. For this type of brim, more material is required than for the former. Therefore, to estimate the exact amount necessary, the best method is to take off a paper pattern of the brim, allowing ½ inch for seam allowances, which will enable you to decide on the width material needed. Twice the amount of the pattern plus ⅝" yard of 18-inch material for the crown will be sufficient for the average-size hat. After the exact amount has been determined in this manner, the material may be cut according to the pattern obtained or it may be applied direct to the frame.

For a narrow roll or a drooping brim, the material may be used on the bias, and the joining then made along the line of the warp or the selvage, the selvage always being cut away.

When fitting fabric with a pile or nap, such as velvet, plush, and duvetyn, apply the fabric to the brim with the pile or nap running to the right, as you hold the front of the hat toward you.

SIMPLICITY TWO-PIECE DRESS

Continued from page 27

Substituting Shirring for Plaits.—If soft material, such as crêpe, is used, the sides may be shirred instead of plaited, as shown in Fig. 13, five or six rows of shirring placed 1 inch apart being desirable. When gathered up, the shirring should take in the allowance of the plait on each side. A loose, long machine stitch permits a quick satisfactory shirring.

Making the Waist-Line Joining.—Next, proceed to pin the skirt to the waist, as shown in Fig. 14, having the edges of the deep plaits, if they are used, meet the under-arm seams. Slip the skirt over the waist with the waist-line edges together, and hold the dress so that you pin the blouse to the skirt, thus preventing its being drawn too tight.

To the notched center front and center back of the skirt, pin the centers of the front and the back of the blouse, and place several pins in between these points. By easing in the waist material, the skirt should fit on very well, but if necessary the plaits may be adjusted slightly.

When the waist and skirt are pinned together, stitch all the way around by machine, using a ⅜-inch seam and overlapping the stitching for a couple of inches. Then overcast the raw edges, as in Fig. 9.

Making the Pocket and Belt.—If pockets are used, finish the upper edge with a center-stitched binding, as in Fig. 15. Turn the lap over to the right side and pin the pockets accurately in position, turning in the edges ⅜ inch. Begin ½ inch from the top, stitch to the top, and then back to stay the top edge securely.

Make a one-inch belt, stitching a fold of material and then turning the material right side. To make a tailored bow for it, cut off a piece of the belt material 5 inches long. Fold the ends over to meet in center, as shown in (a), Fig. 16, and tack down. Cut off another piece 2 inches long, fold this around the first piece at the center, as shown in (b), and tack down, when you will obtain the bow shown in (c).

Sew the tailored bow to one end of the finished belt. If the belt will slip over your shoulders, sew both ends to the bow. If not, put fasteners on the bow and one end of belt. Secure the bow just in front of the left-side seam.

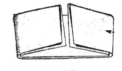

(a)

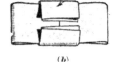

(b)

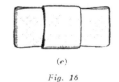

(c)

Fig. 16

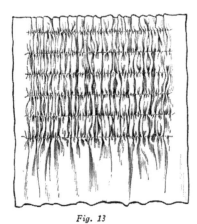

Fig. 13

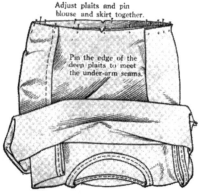

Adjust plaits and pin blouse and skirt together.

Pin the edge of the deep plaits to meet the under-arm seams.

Fig. 14

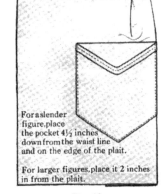

For a slender figure, place the pocket 4½ inches down from the waist line and on the edge of the plait.

For larger figures, place it 2 inches in from the plait.

Fig. 15

Model 13   13 a

THE HOME WOMAN'S MORNING DRESSES

The Discriminating Woman Gives Thought to Good
Lines and Materials Even in Her Home Dresses

Since the dress a woman wears at home, while doing her home work, is a pretty accurate indication of her attitude toward her home and position in it, the discriminating woman, the one who takes pride in the dignity of housework, gives as careful thought to the planning and making of her home dresses as she does to her dinner gowns. She knows the value of good lines, attractive colors, and appropriate materials and their relation to her own figure and coloring. If she is thrifty, as well as discriminating, she knows that she gets better value for her money and more individual dresses if she buys materials and makes her own home dresses. But being thrifty, she does not care to spend long hours on any one dress. She wants designs that are attractive but quickly made. These she will find in pleasing variety in the models shown on Pages 42 and 43.

Model 13.—For the woman who wishes to emphasize a none-too-generous height, striped percale, gingham, or madras is a good choice of material. Further aid to the desired end is the choice of a slenderizing design such as the one here shown. To cut this dress with the set-in sleeves as illustrated, use a pattern, such as Pictorial Review pattern 2272, or for a size above 42, Pictorial Review pattern 2303. For a slender figure, the set-in sleeves are not so essential, and a very similar result may be obtained by using the Straight-Line, One-Piece method of cutting on Page 10. In using the narrow material with this method, put two selvages together instead of the first lengthwise fold of the material mentioned. Arrange two plaits on each hip and stitch them nearly to the bottom of the skirt. Do not shape the front of the neck; merely slash it down, face back the revers, and apply a straight piece of material for the collar. Stickeri braid makes a pleasing finish.

Model 13A.—For the slight, short figure, this model is excellent and may be cut by the Slenderizing One-Piece dress plan, Page 12. For a larger figure, set-in sleeves, as shown in the back view, are more becoming. In that case, a pattern is necessary. McCall pattern 3739 may be used by cutting 1 or 2 inches from each side of the center front and turning back the edges to form the plaits that extend over the edges of the bias central panel.

When set-in sleeves are used, take special care in joining them. Every sleeve pattern cuts the sleeve slightly larger than the armhole it is to fit. Yet it must fit perfectly smooth when completed. In order to do this, gather the sleeve with very tiny stitches and leave the thread loose so that it is adjustable. Put the right sides of the dress and sleeve together, bring the under-arm

seams of the two together, and match the notches. Use plenty of pins at right angles to the edge of the seam. Adjust the fulness so that the sleeve is not full, but merely eased in over the top. Be very careful to keep the lengthwise grain of the sleeve on the top in line with the shoulder seam. Replace the pins with basting, and when it hangs straight, looks well, and "sets" comfortably on the arm, stitch the seam.

In using the Slenderizing One-Piece dress plan of cutting for narrow material, fold one dress length through the center lengthwise, cut it, and insert the bias panel. This will form the center front. The shaping at the under arms will be done on the selvages of the front and back lengths. Since there are no hip plaits, slant the under-arm seam lines very slightly toward the selvage instead of cutting straight to the edge at the waist line.

Model 13B.—This model also is cut on the Slenderizing One-Piece Dress plan. See the suggestions for cutting the slenderizing dress given under Model 13A. In this case, a crosswise panel is used, and the front neck line is not shaped. A straight piece of material attached to the revers forms the collar. The button trimming is attractive, and if desired may actually serve as a means of closing by adding buttonholes. If this is not desired, snaps may be arranged under the plait on the left side.

Model 13C.—For this model with set-in sleeves, use a pattern, such as McCall pattern 3584 or Pictorial Review pattern 2330. The pockets may be real little stand pockets, or imitations, as you prefer.

Model 13D.—Use the Simplicity Two-Piece Dress plan, Page 36, in cutting this quaint basque-like model. A yoke pattern is made by laying the blouse section out flat before the under-arm seams are joined, outlining the neck line on paper, and measuring an even distance from this for the yoke outline. The cuffs are cut slightly circular and of the same width as the yoke.

Model 13E.—The Simplicity Two-Piece plan of cutting is used for this dress. The waist line is quite low, and the skirt fulness is distributed over the hips and back. Sections from the plaid skirt material provide the novel trimming pieces, which have their edges bound with a harmonizing color.

Model 13F.—Use the Slenderizing One-Piece plan for cutting this dress, inserting the front panel before cutting, as suggested for Model 13A. Join the bottom band separately.

SMARTNESS KEYNOTES HOME DRESSES

The narrow front panel of Model 13B is joined to the dress with the same stitching that holds the plaits at each side of it. Striped gingham, percale, or novelty cotton material makes up well in this way. The collar and cuffs can be white or a plain color.

Plaid gingham with blue as the predominant color is the choice for Model 13C. Plain blue Everfast is used for the trimmings. The pockets are merely imitations made of double pieces, stitched at the ends and lower edge.

A rather full skirt of plain Everfast with a broad band of cretonne applied to its lower edge is joined to a cretonne blouse with plain yoke and cuffs in Model 13D. It is a good model for a tall, slender figure.

That a practical combination like gingham and Everfast can be pretty is proved by Model 13E, which takes advantage of the lines of the plaid in cutting its trimmings. The edges of these plaid triangles are bound with a harmonizing color, which is also used for binding the neck line. The slight fulness of the skirt adds to its comfort.

The woman who enjoys wearing browns and tans will welcome the thought of using these tones in Everfast for her morning dress. Model 13F suggests a pleasant combination of the two colors. Plain seams are used in joining the brown bands down the front and at the bottom. The belt slips through openings at the front and ties in the back.

14 C

14 A

14 B

14 D

14 E

Model 14

14 F

14 G

LINGERIE KEEPS IN LINE WITH OUTERWEAR

Divergence From the Reigning Simplicity is Felt in the Use of Much Lace

Model 14.—The treasured slimness of the straight-line silhouette owes much to the costume slip that is planned to avoid bulk while supplying the ease necessary for comfort. A clever solution of the problem is shown in this model, which requires a minimum amount of material, three lengths providing two slips for the average figure. The diagonal hip darts provide ease in the back.

Pin one full width of material around the back of the figure or dress form, shaping it slightly from the waist line to the top to get a straight line where it joins the front panel.

For the panel, use half a width of material folded through the center lengthwise. Measure off 2 inches from the lengthwise edges at the top, cutting the sides in a slanting direction from this point so that the panel will be 4 inches wider at the bottom than at the top. The hip darts are 1 inch deep and 13 or 14 inches long. For some figures, better results are obtained by slanting them diagonally downward in the back rather than upward, as shown.

Model 14A.—Double folds of cream net hemstitched to the edges of orchid crêpe de Chine add the newest touch of daintiness to these step-ins. Quaint posies of the crêpe, blind-stitched to the net, give the much-sought "different" look.

Cut the top straight with a seam under each arm or use a lengthwise piece going around, making sure that it is as wide as the hip measure because this is a step-in garment. The lower part may be cut either straight or circular. If it is cut straight, the center-front and center-back seams are not necessary. The sides are left open and edged with double folds of net hemstitched in place. Gather any fulness at the top of the lower section and join it to the camisole top with a French seam.

Model 14B.—Cut both front and back of this dainty white batiste model with a slight flare toward the lower edge. The top, when finished, should be 1 or 2 inches larger than the bust measure. Allow an additional 2 inches for front fulness, gathering this to fit the lace, which may be any odd bit of filet or similar lace. Apply the tiny ends of insertion and have the top band, which is cut separately, hemstitched on. Two lengths of material are sufficient.

Model 14C.—Two lengths of peach crêpe de Chine or pink batiste, 2 yards of wide lace, such as filet, baby Irish, or Alencon, and 1 yard of narrow edging supply the necessary materials for this lovely gown, which takes its inspiration from the outerwear fashions.

Fold the material crosswise 1 inch from the center to give more length to the front. Allow for the group of tiny tucks that run over the shoulder. Then cut off a narrow wedge-shaped piece from each side, tapering it out to the selvage at the lower edge. The width of this piece at the top must be decided for the individual figure. For the neck opening, make a 9-inch slit in the exact center of the crosswise fold. From the center of the slit, cut down the center front 8 or 10 inches. Lay back the lapels and apply a straight piece of lace for the collar.

Model 14D.—Voile is so intrinsically dainty that it can afford to lend itself to a more or less tailored design. When worn with a pair of bloomers, the chemise shown completes a pretty two-piece set. It is particularly feminine when the body of the garment is white and the shaped top portion is pale pink with lavender or pale-green ribbon bows. Cut a paper pattern for the shaped top, allowing 1 or 2 inches more than the bust measure for ease. Cut the voile top double with a fold at the upper edge. It may be joined with entre deux or machine hemstitching.

Model 14E.—Crêpe de Chine, radium silk, or tricolette, in navy with rust-color trimmings, or in rust with navy trimmings, is a pleasing and practical choice for the dark costume slip.

To make the slip from a minimum amount of material, add 6 inches to the bust measure and buy twice that amount. Cut the material into two equal lengths, one of which will be used for the skirt front. Cut the other one lengthwise so that one of the pieces is as wide as you want the depth of the camisole. Use the remaining piece for the back panel of the skirt. Arrange most of the fulness over the hips. Feather-stitching adds a light touch to the trimming.

Model 14F.—To simplify the problems of her toilet, the tiny girl will appreciate this dainty garment, which slips on over her head and needs no buttons. It is made from a length of embroidery flouncing shaped under each arm and gathered slightly into narrow bands hemstitched on at the top. Shoulder straps and narrow lace edging complete the slip.

Model 14G.—For the older child who can manage buttons with creditable finesse, this quaint slip is designed. A straight piece of batiste makes the bodice top, which buttons in the back, and another straight piece forms the skirt. Dainty lace insertion is applied in an unusual way as decoration.

NEGLIGEES HOLD TO SIMPLE, GRACEFUL LINES

For the Lighter Hours of Leisure, There
Are Dainty Robes Inviting Relaxation

Model 15.—A charming adaptation of the Japanese kimono is shown in this lovely negligée of silk crêpe or satin with soft marabou bandings.

Two lengths, or about 3 yards, of 40-inch material is required. Cut a strip 10 inches wide from the full length of the material at one side. This, when cut in half crosswise, supplies the draped sleeves. Fold the remaining 30-inch-wide piece, crosswise, through the center. Place a pin 2 inches to one side of the fold so that the front will be slightly longer than the back. Slit the front lengthwise through the center from the lower edge to the pin. Shape the neck line from the end of the slash to a point about 12 inches below. If the body of the garment extends out too far on the shoulder, shape it by cutting in a slightly diagonal line toward the lower edge of the garment. The sleeves are sewed to the body part in a deep armhole effect. Join all sleeve edges in a plain seam, so as to form deep pocket-like sleeves. The tie and belt may be made of ribbon or of self-material.

Model 15A.—For a practical and becoming kimono made on simple lines, this model could hardly be surpassed. The cutting and making, too, are very simple.

The kimono requires for the average figure 3 yards for length and ¾ yard for the sleeves. Remove the ¾-yard sleeve allowance, slitting the remaining material on the lengthwise fold for the center-front opening. This slit should extend 2 inches more than half the length. Then shape the neck line, making it round in the back and a deep V in the front, as indicated. Gore off the sides very slightly, cutting about 3 inches from the selvage at the shoulder and gradually slanting them to the edge near the bottom. Shape the sleeves as directed for the sleeves of the Straight-Line, One-Piece dress. Make them wider for the negligée, however, than you would for the dress. In applying the sleeve, match the point with the point on the shoulder and join with plain or French seams. Then sew up the under-arm seams and apply the trimming bands. Hem the bottom.

This type of garment is well suited to development in heavy materials, such as corduroy and blanket cloth.

Model 15B.—This youthful negligée can be made very readily by the most inexperienced seamstress, as it has but two seams and three bound edges. It is made from two straight pieces of material, the full width being used in the upper portion and the lengthwise grain being used around the body for the skirt.

To find the length required for the upper part, measure from a low waist line in front, over the shoulder, and down to a corresponding point in the back. Fold a width of material of this length crosswise through the center and shape the neck line, cutting it lower in front than in back.

Measure from the low waist line down the length desired for the skirt. If the material is wider than the skirt length desired, turn up a hem, or cut a strip from one edge and leave the opposite selvage as a finish for the bottom. Make the straight skirt 15 or 20 inches wider than the hip measure, arranging the one seam to come on the left side where it is very inconspicuous. Join the skirt section to the top in a plain seam.

Bind the sleeve openings and the neck line. If desired, a very pleasing note may be added by using a contrasting color in the binding. Tie a ribbon around the waist and finish it with ribbon posies edged with lace.

Model 15C.—A negligée of cream lace and pale salmon-pink Georgette over a straight little slip of soft green crêpe de Chine envelopes Milady with a fairy-like charm. Or, if she is the type to wear blue lace, pink slip, and orchid chiffon, the resultant charm is not decreased.

Make a straight costume slip of soft green crêpe de Chine and tack a length of wide lace to the front, catching it to the shoulder straps. Cut the Georgette 30 inches longer than the finished length desired for the negligée. Have all the edges picoted, run a row of hemstitching up 30 inches from the lower edge directly through the center, and split the hemstitching so that it forms a picoted edge on each side of the split material. Drape the end that was not split over the shoulders, as shown, catching it and the lace to the shoulder straps with tiny rosebuds. You may shape the material at the back of the neck if desired. Otherwise, it will lie in soft folds. Now drape up the lower corners of the Georgette and tack them to the lace with buds. The 30-inch row of hemstitching that was split to form the picot edging now forms the lower edge of the drape. Tack the draperies invisibly wherever they need it to hang well. The negligée slips over the head.

Model 15D.—Simplicity and comfort combine to make this combing jacket desirable. It is cut from a 36-inch square of challis or crêpe de Chine. Fold the square diagonally through the center and slash it on the fold to a point 3 inches beyond the center. Then, at the end of this slash and at right angles to it, cut 3 inches to the right and an equal distance to the left to provide the neck opening and lapels. The cuffs are made by folding back the side corners. Bind all edges with ribbon and tack the edges together under the arms. The only fastening is a ribbon tie.

Model 15

15 C

15 a

15 B

15 D

Look for a collectible print version at the end of this issue.

Magic Pattern: *Heart Shaped Apron*

This is an original Magic Pattern, a project you cut out using diagrams instead of pattern pieces. These were first created by Mary Brooks Picken for the Woman's Institute's student magazines, Inspiration and Fashion Service. My book **Vintage Notions: An Inspirational Guide to Needlework, Cooking, Sewing, Fashion & Fun** *featured 12 original Magic Patterns. Recently I have created modern patterns that were inspired by these vintage gems featured in the book* **The Magic Pattern Book**, *which I licensed with Workman Publishing. We have chosen to keep the authenticity of this original pattern intact and therefore have not changed instructions based on modern fabrics and techniques. Note at the end of this pattern you will find helpful tips for drafting pattern pieces.*

▶▶▶ A HEART-SHAPED apron has quite obviously a bit of sentiment about it that disguises its practical, domestic, easy-to-iron character. This attractive apron is made from ¾ yd. of 40-in. gingham, with a package of bias tape and matching thread for finishing.

To cut: Straighten fabric. Tear off two crosswise strips 2 in. wide for band and strings. Place fold of apron piece next to you, as in the diagram. Measure up from point A 13½ in. to B. Measure to right of B 16 in.; place C. Draw a curved line from C to corner D for bottom of apron.

Place E 3¼ in. above B. Measure across 9½ in. to locate F. Draw a curved line for the bottom of pocket, as shown. Chalk straight from G down 5 in. to H. Shape the bib as shown, by slanting line to I, then curving around end rather deeply. Cut out apron after it is chalked on fabric. Cut B through C to D for apron part. Then cut pocket and bib.

To make: Seam selvages of the bib pieces together on right side, using a ⅛-in. seam. Clip selvages at intervals of about 1 in. along their full length. Press seam open and cover it with seam binding. Notch a point at top center of each heart curve. Then notch waist about 2 in. from center-front on each side. Stitch bias binding from notch to notch.

Hem tops of pockets, turning ¼ in.; then 1½ in. Bind edges of pockets. Bind outside edge of apron and sides and top of heart bib. Gather waistline of apron for band. Seam two selvages of strips together. Place this seam at center of waistline; stitch band in position, using ¼-in. seam. Turn raw edges and ends of band in all the way and stitch them.

Turn bottom of bib over ¼ in. on right side; stitch this behind waistband, centering bib at center-front of apron. Pin pockets in position, as shown in sketch, and stitch them in place, turning and stitching back about 1 in. at top of each so that edges cannot pull out.

Sew small safety pins under the side bands at top of bib to pin to your dress, or use two decorative scatter pins.

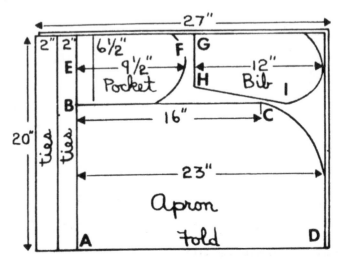

Your Measurement Chart & Notes on Making Magic Patterns

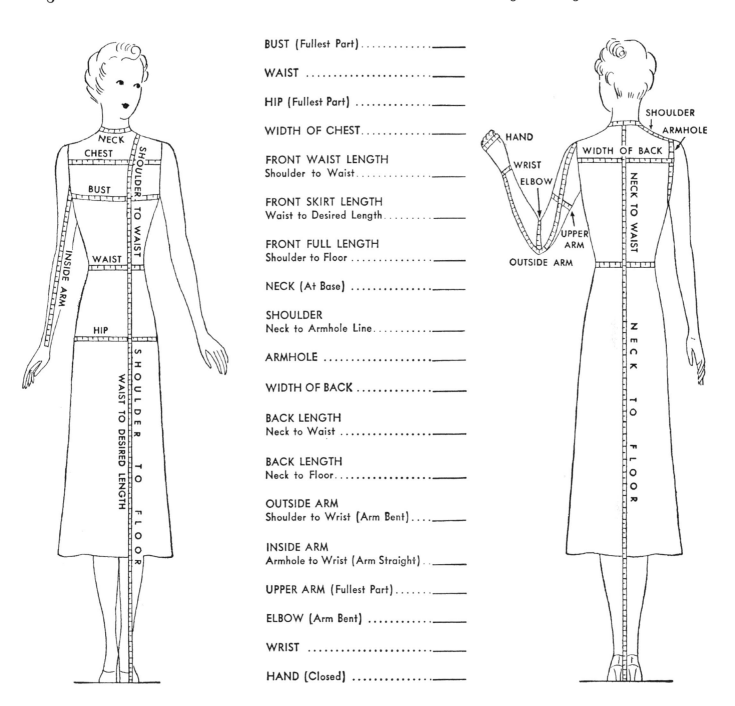

BUST (Fullest Part)............._____

WAIST ...._____

HIP (Fullest Part) ...._____

WIDTH OF CHEST............._____

FRONT WAIST LENGTH
Shoulder to Waist.............._____

FRONT SKIRT LENGTH
Waist to Desired Length........._____

FRONT FULL LENGTH
Shoulder to Floor ...._____

NECK (At Base) ...._____

SHOULDER
Neck to Armhole Line..........._____

ARMHOLE ...._____

WIDTH OF BACK ...._____

BACK LENGTH
Neck to Waist ...._____

BACK LENGTH
Neck to Floor................._____

OUTSIDE ARM
Shoulder to Wrist (Arm Bent)...._____

INSIDE ARM
Armhole to Wrist (Arm Straight)..._____

UPPER ARM (Fullest Part)......._____

ELBOW (Arm Bent) ...._____

WRIST ...._____

HAND (Closed) ...._____

Keep Accurate Measurements

Since the garments in this book are all cut from measurements, it is necessary to have accurate ones to follow. Keep a list of your own measurements always at hand for ready reference.

Measurements for fitted garments should be taken over the type of foundation garments you expect to wear with them. Remove dress, jacket, or coat, which would distort the measurements. Do not take measurements too tight. Make all easy enough for comfort. The chart shows how to place the tape correctly for each measurement.

Making The Pattern

If you have the least doubt about your ability to chalk out the garment on your fabric, then rough it out first with crayon or heavy pencil on wrapping paper or newspaper. Cut out the paper pattern and use it to cut your garment. Cutting from a diagram, you can be sure that the proportions are correct for your size and that the garment will be a good fit.

Look for a collectible print version at the end of this issue.

THE SECRETS OF DISTINCTIVE DRESS

CHAPTER III

APPROPRIATE DRESS

STATION IN LIFE—OCCASION—SEASON—SHOES AND HOSE—HATS, VEILS, AND GLOVES—THE WEARING OF FURS—THE WEARING OF JEWELRY—THE WEARING OF FLOWERS—DRESSING APPROPRIATELY—CULTIVATING INTELLIGENCE IN DRESS—A CLOTHES TRIUMPH.

Much has been written on the subject of "station in life." In the older countries marked distinction exists between people of wealth and rank and the peasantry.

In France, the peasant women delight in wearing their caps and aprons; in fact, it is almost an unheard-of thing for peasant women to be without them, for they take great pride in honest toil and want it known that they are "in service."

In America, there are no such class distinctions. Here daughters from every country are blended in the making of American women; but even in this great Democracy appropriateness of dress should be understood and observed.

If your position in life is such that you are looked up to and respected by your friends and

Originally published in *The Secrets of Distinctive Dress, 1918*

the community at large, you should be careful almost to a point of fastidiousness in the matter of clothes. Regardless of where you live or how many people you meet in the day, there are some who may be affected by your knowledge and appreciation of dress or your lack of it. For this reason, if for no other, you should be exceedingly careful to give no one a chance to misjudge or criticize you.

We never know what effect our example will have on our associates. To enjoy peace of mind and do our part well, we should make sure that our conduct and morals are above reproach and our style of dressing beyond criticism. For the woman of moderate means to be well dressed entails no hardships, for dignified economy and good taste invariably go hand in hand.

When we see a young girl or a woman dressed in extravagant fineries and we know that her income or that of her father or her husband is too small to support such a display, we cannot help but pity her and often, unfortunately, question her integrity. No woman should place herself in a position where she will be the object of undeserved sympathy or suspicion.

There are some men who look on all womankind as a bundle of lace and ribbon, and measure their business intelligence by this standard. This is unfair and the pity is that those responsible for it are women who are unable to discriminate where feminine finery is concerned. Nothing is more exquisitely feminine and attractive than fluffy lace and dainty ribbon used in the right place and at the right time, and nothing more unattractive than the display of such finery in inappropriate surroundings.

The love of pretty clothes causes many girls much unhappiness. Every girl should be taught from earliest childhood the value of the right kinds of clothes, as well as when and where to wear garments of certain types.

If girls are taught early in life the principles of correct dress and the value of strict adherence to the rules of correct dressing, they will not appear at the office in the morning with a hat that is appropriate only for afternoon or evening wear, with thin silk stockings, with chiffon blouses, and an excess of jewelry; rather, they will prize these things enough to keep them for the proper occasion, and, for the office, wear clothes that are comfortable, practical, and appropriate—clothes that will make it possible for them to give a good full day of intelligent service.

Many club women and others interested in civic affairs have discussed the possibility of trying to teach young girls in offices and shops appropriateness in dress.

Usually, such efforts, after investigation, come to naught, simply because these enthusiasts realize that dress is largely an individual problem, one that no corporation or firm can handle, except by making iron-clad rules, which usually result in a uniform.

This, though economical from the individual's point of view, is not desirable nor practical for small offices and institutions. Rather, in such places, it is better to display individuality in one's attire with good taste as the distinguishing feature.

A new era in woman's clothes is dawning, or, rather, a new outlook has been acquired by many. In factories and public places where women are employed to do the work of men, they wear bloomers and Russian blouses; or, sometimes, they wear full hip trousers, leggings, and a coat that gives the costume the appearance of a riding habit.

Such costumes are appropriate if worn when necessity demands. They should be chosen discreetly, however, as a woman's figure differs from that of a man. Such a costume should be full enough over the hips and thighs and correctly fitted over the bust to avoid emphasizing the presence of flesh.

If a woman's work is such as to demand a mannish costume, there is no reason why she should not wear it with comfort and grace and be just as much a gentlewoman as she would be in the most feminine costume. A real gentlewoman never needs to tell you that she is a gentlewoman. Her presence speaks more convincingly than words.

OCCASION

A great number of magazine articles have dwelt at length upon appropriateness in dress, and especially appropriate dress for all occasions; yet, with all that has been written and said upon this interesting and far-reaching subject, we see on every hand and on all occasions costumes that make the wearers conspicuous because of their inappropriateness.

For example, at an informal gathering of young women, all simply attired—most of them wore their business dresses, as it was a business meeting held in the early evening—one young woman came in a low neck, sleeveless evening gown. She was conspicuous, and doubtless was most uncomfortable. Had it not been for the level-headedness of the other young women present, the appearance of this

gay butterfly in the midst of these busy young bees might have caused a serious mental disturbance, as the meeting had been called for the discussion of personal development.

Another time, I was disturbed to see a young woman hastening across the street, a market street it was, in sleeved apron and boudoir cap—a fussy, lacy cap that would have been pretty in her bedroom, but words are inadequate to express its "out-of-placeness" on a public thoroughfare.

Another example: In a dietetics class held in the forenoon in a classroom, a young woman of good family wore a bedraggled afternoon dress, doubtless with the thought of wearing it out and getting as much good out of it as possible. The dress was distracting to the other members of the class, and the criticism she subjected herself to was costly—more costly than a simple businesslike dress befitting the occasion.

When we learn, as a people, to take the matter of dress seriously and conscientiously, study it as we would the subject of food for the table or reading matter for the development of the intellect, we will have removed ourselves from the pale of criticism and will be appreciated for the common sense and good taste expressed in our attire.

SEASON

One's physical comfort frequently keeps a very good check on appropriate dress for the season. For instance, on a midsummer's day, particularly in the warm climate of the Southern and Central States, it is rare to see a dress of wool, especially of a dark color, except when worn through necessity. Not many years ago, however, if a woman had one black woolen dress (or possibly it was silk), it served for church service every Sunday in the year, and was also due to serve for the Fourth-of-July celebration.

Elderly mothers have come to realize that they look ten years younger and are ten times more comfortable on a warm summer's day in a pretty, soft white dress, and it is pleasing to see a group of such mothers dressed in pretty, light wash dresses, as they appear many times as attractive as a group of young women.

For summer wear in offices, a low-necked and short-sleeved frock, with inadequate petticoats, no matter how pleasing the color or how pretty the design or how becoming, is not appropriate.

A simple frock of modest design and coloring, with a dainty, yet dignified, neck and reasonably short sleeves and adequate petticoats

—one with a double front—is entirely appropriate. In fact, such a frock is pleasing and comfortable for business, provided both dress and petticoats are absolutely clean.

Milliners, dressmakers, and merchants, to offset the lull after Christmas, begin showing spring suits and spring hats, and it is not uncommon to see in the coldest days of January a straw hat and low shoes, and in the warmest days of July, furs and, frequently, heavy hats of velvet and fur. Pages and pages condemning this practice have appeared in trade papers and magazines, but it is becoming so established that sometimes one feels almost conspicuous in a winter hat after the first of February and in a summer hat after the middle of July.

This condition should not exist, because it is illogical and inconsistent. Such practices create business for the milliners and merchants at the expense of women who are martyrs to fashion. The only way this condition can be adjusted is for every woman to be a law unto herself regarding the wearing of out-of-season clothes.

The buying of cheap clothes is false economy. Buy good, conservative clothes, take care of them, and wear them more than one season, if necessary.

When spring comes and the winter coat, hat, and furs are to be put away, brush them, clean them thoroughly, and take care to store them where they will not become unduly wrinkled. When clothes become too wrinkled, it is almost impossible to get them to look presentable again. The most careful steaming and pressing usually fails to restore them to their original condition.

In hanging clothes away, place them carefully on hangers in clothes sacks in your closet, so that they will be safe from dust and in good condition when you have occasion to wear them. To guard against damage from moths, put moth preventives in the sack.

Before you buy your next winter's outfit, get out these things you have carefully put away and see what repairing and remodeling are necessary to make them wearable.

You will be surprised to find how much better your things will look than you had anticipated and how frequently you can save many dollars by making use of some of your last season's clothes.

In the winter, it is frequently convenient to wear little summer dresses about the house. However, if your summer dresses are not to be worn during the winter, wash them free of starch and put them away in bags or boxes.

Garments made of white material should be put into a light-colored bag that has been thoroughly blued so that they will not become yellow.

Summer hats are rarely wearable the second season, unless they are of good straw or braid and can be reblocked or redyed. But a hat, be it a summer or a winter one, should be put away with care, because, frequently, there are trimmings that can be utilized in making a new hat or for some other purpose.

SHOES AND HOSE

A neat shoe is a necessity for a tiny foot. How distressing it is to see an attractive foot in a shabby or unkempt shoe. And a large foot—well, it must of necessity be well-shod, shod in a way that will not attract attention to it.

When buying shoes, always have your foot measured. Do not try to give your size and insist upon having it, because you may have gained or lost flesh, and this gain or loss is evident on your foot the same as on your hands or any other part of the body. Then, too, shoes manufactured by different firms are made on different lasts, and the same size-number may be larger or smaller, according to the last used.

Shoes should never be tight. Tight shoes cause many ills, and no one can ever appear graceful or at ease in a shoe that is uncomfortable.

It is economical as well as comfortable to have several pairs of shoes, as it rests the feet to wear different shoes. The leather frequently is softer in one pair than in another and consequently the feet are made a little more comfortable by the change.

Much is added to the attractiveness of a costume if proper shoes are worn.

In selecting shoes to wear with certain dresses, exercise care to have the leather of the shoes correspond with the texture of the dress. For instance, soft silk dresses, such as charmeuse and satin, are really better with low fine kid or patent-leather shoes, and, the shoes being low, silk stockings help to soften the lines of the foot.

Patent-leather shoes, oxfords, and slippers are frequently desirable for wear with lingerie dresses, as well as with silk and satin dresses.

If it is not practicable to wear low shoes, cloth-top shoes or very fine kid-top shoes with light soles are in good taste. There are times, however, when "cloth tops" cannot be procured, even though they do seem to be more agreeable for soft dresses.

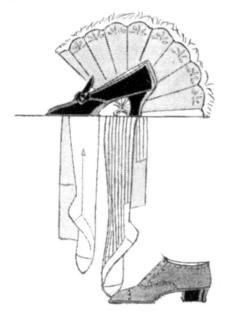

The hard-surface woolen materials, such as heavy cheviots, serges, tweeds, and novelty suitings, seem to call for shoes of reasonably heavy leather, usually dark tan, brown, or black.

The wearing of button or lace shoes is usually controlled by fashion. When lace shoes are in fashion, it is almost impossible to purchase button shoes, and vice versa.

Remember that, in the house, the heavy shoes you have worn on the street are not appropriate, especially if you change to a house dress. Besides, if you establish the habit of changing from street shoes to house shoes while you are in the house, your feet and your shoes will be better for it, and you will enjoy much greater comfort.

We should cultivate a little of the English woman's accuracy in wearing the right thing at the right time.

A tailored suit calls for a shoe with a plain heel, not by any means a French heel. Some women, in their desire to appear appropriately dressed, wear a low-heeled walking shoe with their tailored suits and a French heel with their afternoon and evening gowns. This practice cannot be carried out without serious results, because changing the position of the foot weakens the arches, causes considerable strain, tires the feet, and frequently causes swelling.

Physicians disagree about the wearing of high- and low-heeled shoes.

It seems logical that a reasonably low heel gives greater comfort and is more sensible, but the high heels have had the favor of the majority for so long a time that they have come to be a factor that must be reckoned with, even though condemned by our most eminent physicians. High heels are considered attractive, because they seem to make the foot appear smaller and to add a little to a woman's height.

Common sense tells us that the low heels are better; our pride argues that the high heels look better on us. Then why not strike a happy medium and wear a heel that is not too high nor too low?

Heels one and one-half or one and seven-eighths inches high cannot do any injury, and they are usually more attractive than lower heels. The heel height of one's shoes should be uniform, so that the feet will always be in the same position.

A woman's hose should match her shoes in color, and black hose should be worn with black shoes. Unless your dress is white or light-colored, do not wear light-colored or white hose with dark shoes.

HATS, VEILS, AND GLOVES

We talk of clothes making a background for us, of having our dresses made of a color that harmonizes with our individuality, and even of having our coat linings of such a color that when they are thrown back on our chair they add to the background of the picture. But do we realize fully the value of the right hat—the individual hat, the hat that makes a background for our eyes, our face, our hair?

The greatest dress artists say: "Dress to the eyes; if the eyes are not definite enough in color, dress to the hair, not forgetting the contour of the face."

We must expect a great deal from our hats. They must make a frame for the face. The kindliness and good cheer, the spirit of life, that our faces express for us must have a fitting background. If we are not in our homes, then our hats must be intimate enough to make a desirable background.

If plain dresses and plain suits, i. e., tailored frocks and suits, are becoming to you, you will almost invariably find that tailored hats are becoming.

Pretty-faced girls and women with luxuriant hair may wear small hats well. Usually, faces in which no lines have formed and the kindly face of the mother, with lines that mean a very great deal, may also have a small hat as a background. But the "in-between" woman, with lines showing in her face when it does not seem quite time for them, should wear a hat that has enough brim to overshadow the lines.

It has been said that the woman who has lines in her face should try to have hats with dark facings, because a light facing in her hat will allow every line to show and make the face less attractive.

Some women can wear an all-white hat with a white dress, for the reflection coming up from the dress will soften the lines enough to make the white hat agreeable and becoming.

When you are buying a hat, try a number on. Look at them from the front, the back, and the sides, and study their lines and coloring intelligently. Walk about with the hat on. Sometimes, when you are sitting, the hat may be very pretty, but when you stand you may find that you are too tall or not tall enough for that shape of hat.

Never buy a hat hastily nor without considering whether it is becoming to your face, whether it is suitable for your hair, or whether it is agreeable in color and appropriate for

wear with the garments, suits, or dresses that you have. If the hat is to be worn with some particular suit or coat, have that garment on, so that exactly the right effect may be attained. Remember that much of the smartness of your costume depends on your hat. You should give it great consideration and be sure that it is right for you in every particular.

At some time you may have been so disappointed with a certain shape of hat that you continually avoid getting a hat of that kind again. Perhaps, though, there was some particular line or color that made it unbecoming; so, when the opportunity presents itself, do not hesitate to try on a hat of a similar shape, because you may find one that is becoming.

Another thing to remember is that if you gain or lose weight you may have to change the shape of your hat. A shape that is desirable for a slender figure is not agreeable for a stout one, and the shape that you wore at twenty may not be becoming when you are thirty or forty.

Beautiful picture hats, especially those of black and dark colors, are wonderful in the right place—at a fashionable restaurant, a hotel dining room, or an afternoon social function—but they are not suitable for business or street wear.

Faded flowers, bedraggled feathers, and crumpled chiffons are not pleasing in hats.

Veils, like perfume, are an exquisite luxury, if they are dainty, delicate, and becoming. Beautiful veils can cover a "multitude of sins," and rarely are they ugly.

Veils sometimes seem out of place; at other times they seem straggly. However, if they are worn for a reason—to enhance the beauty of the hat, to give the appearance of a complete toilet, to protect the face, all logical reasons—then they are very desirable.

Always wear veils with care and discrimination. They should be of a color and weave that you know will add to your attractiveness, and they should not be so heavy, unless they are for motoring or outing, as to conceal your features.

In purchasing and wearing veils, follow fashion dictations as far as is logical, for frequently very smart effects may be produced by the addition of a veil.

Gloves, romantic, yet necessary articles of wear, like dainty handkerchiefs, bespeak the nicest niceties of the wearer. Gloves should always be in accord with the costume, and—always clean and carefully fitted. Fine kid gloves are delightful possessions, but they are more extravagant than washable kid, lisle, or

silk. Kid gloves with furs, silk gloves with lingerie dresses, is a rule that can be followed out with surety.

THE WEARING OF FURS

Character seems to be expressed to a very great extent in furs. We all seem to know the woman who wears beaver, mole, skunk, fox, mink, sable, and ermine. Every woman has her preference as to fur, and you can usually wear the fur that you like best, provided you combine it with suitable material or arrange the shaping so that it is becoming to you.

An aristocratic young woman, slender and graceful, with hair that is beautifully dressed and a gown that has attractive coloring, may, if her pocketbook permits, wear ermine.

Women from thirty to fifty can wear scarfs of mole to splendid advantage, especially if it is combined with the darkest American-Beauty shades or with a color or a material that will give life to supplant the lack of color in the mole skin.

Skunk, red fox, and any of the long-haired furs should not be worn by any person who is not absolutely tidy in every particular. Straggly hair, irregular skirt and coat lengths, and a draggly get-up do not combine well with long-haired furs. In such a case, a short-haired, compact fur piece will be more attractive, because it will help to give neatness rather than emphasize the lack of it.

Some dress artists say that heads on furs are extremely poor taste and should never be worn. This is largely a matter of individual taste. Personally, I should not enjoy the heads, because there is a soft familiarity about furs which I like and which, I fear, the animal heads might take away.

Furs are beautiful, and if you wear them in the right place with the right effect, they will actually *make* a costume. But when you wear them just because you possess them, without regard to place or costume, you err against one of the fine principles of dress and openly insult one of the most beautiful of our dress accessories.

If you possess furs that were not selected especially for your requirements and in accord with your individuality, do not consider them hopeless. If they are good furs, go to a dependable furrier and try on furs from his stock until you find a shape and size that is becoming. Then, see what you can do about altering your furs to assume a similar shaping. Satin of excellent quality and of a color that is suitable can very frequently be combined with fur in a delightful way.

If your furs are more valuable, and possibly more becoming, than you feel your suit will be, plan your suit to bring out the beauty of the furs.

Furs should enrich costume, never detract from it. They should give evidence of "luxurious warmth"—a very good reason why you should not wear them on July Fourth or on an August day, unless, of course, you are in a climate where the warmth of a soft beautiful fur gives comfort in midsummer.

THE WEARING OF JEWELRY

Usually, jewelry is given to us; rarely is it purchased for our particular requirements. Somebody wants to give us something very pretty and gives us jewelry that appeals to him or to her, seldom taking into consideration whether it harmonizes with our individuality or not.

This is a pity, because jewelry is one thing that seems convenient to give to those we care a great deal for. If we must give jewelry, we should use great care in selecting it, so that the person who is to receive it can wear it comfortably and feel that it is appropriate.

A dear mother whom I know possesses a pair of earrings and a lavaliere that would be pretty on a girl of eighteen or twenty, but they detract so much from the mother's dignity that, to be a real friend, you would feel that you should tell her of their inappropriateness for her. But she treasures them dearly, because they are gifts of two sons that she loves very much. It is evident that she has never considered whether or not she should wear them, but has worn them almost continually because her loved ones gave them to her.

I appreciate sentiment so much that I should hesitate to tell this mother that she should not wear these pieces of jewelry, but in conformity with the rules of appropriate dress one has to say definitely that she should not.

It is said that only brilliant women—that is, intelligent women who are beautifully gowned and handsome both as to face and figure—should wear diamonds, because their very being should sparkle in company with the beautiful stones; yet the joy that one feels in the possession of even one beautiful stone seems like a sufficient excuse to warrant the wearing of diamonds by every person who can afford them.

But, again, if we are to practice the correct rules of dress and apply them persistently to ourselves, we must persist in sacrifice, and sometimes this means sacrificing the very things we like best. To be beautiful, attrac-

Select Pictures *Photo by Alfred Cheney Johnston*

NORMA TALMADGE

Unique or unusual jewelry is always interesting, especially when worn by
such a delightfully unusual person as Miss Talmadge

tive, and appropriately dressed is a serious undertaking, but you can be all this if you make persistency your watchword.

Many ultrarich women own exquisite jewels, and frequently they wear them because they possess them, and not because the jewels are appropriate. On the other hand, many do wear jewels with due regard to their place and decorative value.

A string of pearls can enhance a soft, lacy costume and add a great deal to its attractiveness and individual becomingness. Pearls can be worn, too, with exquisite soft velvets and satins, but they require a fitting background to make them most beautiful.

I once knew a woman who wore topazes in simple plain settings with her brown costumes. She had brown hair and brown eyes, and the topazes added just enough life to her costumes to make them decidedly fetching. Another woman I knew wore corals with soft gray and another wore amethysts with pink-tans and pink-grays, combinations that added to their attractiveness. The dresses with which these jewels were worn were simple in design and not overtrimmed, thus giving the jewels decorative value—a chance to brighten the costumes and to express individuality in a delightful way.

A graceful string of jet black beads frequently adds just the right touch to a costume that seems a flat mass of color and needs something to add smartness to it. Corals and pearl beads also may be used for the same purpose, but they should be used with a color that they either subdue or brighten.

I want you to understand my meaning here. For instance, a turquoise evening gown of satin that seems a mass of brilliant color may be subdued by the addition of a string of black beads that give line to the gown and help to quiet the color. On the other hand, black jet beads worn with a lusterless black gown will brighten it.

A brooch should not be worn for mere adornment. It should have a purpose and be used at the termination of the neck line or to hold some part of the costume in place. It should not be placed on the gown merely because you possess it and desire to wear it.

I recall a sewing class in which we openly discussed correct and incorrect dress. After having weekly meetings for a year, I felt that the entire membership was well informed as to correct and incorrect dress, and I was proud to meet any member, because each expressed the little niceties of dress we had tried to instil and cultivate.

One woman, I remember quite distinctly, seemed deeply impressed with what had been said about jewels, and, with means at her command, insisted on wearing jewelry that harmonized with her costumes. She took particular pains to harmonize them in color, because she seemed to have this point definitely in mind, but she entirely lost sight of the shape and appropriateness of the jewelry.

She was a frail creature with little color, and we had decided by experiment that deep red (burgundy) was the most appropriate color for her. She had seen a demonstration of a brown-and-topaz combination and was thrilled by the beauty of it, so she proceeded to buy a very dark-red velvet dress, deep and rich in color and beautiful in texture. Then she purchased a garnet necklace arranged in a heavy gold mounting, the gold taking away the beauty of the red velvet and making the garnet so hard and unfriendly that it seemed to be an absolute stranger to her—a thing we should never permit in anything that we wear.

Our clothes—every stitch, even our handkerchiefs—should express our individuality, express us in the most beautiful way possible.

The necklace that I have mentioned cost considerable money, and it took courage to say to my friend:

"Don't you think the pearls you have would be better for wear with your velvet gown? I am sure I should like them better, because they would be 'more friendly' to you. They would give the softness and whiteness at the neck that your gown needs."

Always remember that the jewelry you wear must be worn with consideration, not to make you appear as if you were advertising a cheap jewelry establishment.

Always ask yourself: Does the piece of jewelry add to the appearance of my gown? Does it seem to have a place there? Would a person in looking at me see my gown first and then find the jewels there as a part of the gown, or would the jewels stand out as being merely adornment and not a part of the color scheme or line effect that I wish my gown to express for me?

I have always been a believer in wearing good things, feeling that cheap clothes, cheap jewels, cheap anything, express cheapness of person and "cheapness of mentality"; and rather than have cheap jewels, I would not have any. But I have frequently had gowns where a little inexpensive brooch, or sometimes a string of beads, was just the right color, size, and shape to add to the beauty of the gown and make it seem more complete.

There are many shops that sell inexpensive things that are exquisite in workmanship. Frequently, copies of beautiful pieces of jewelry, which can be worn during the life of a gown, can be bought for a reasonable sum, and then they can be laid aside for some future time without a feeling of loss.

Of course, if a woman knows that brown, gray, purple, white, or black is her particular color and she always wears this color in the majority, she frequently can afford to purchase jewels that are rare in quality and beautiful in design, because she will need so few when she holds definitely to one color scheme and similar style.

Another precaution about wearing jewelry: Do not wear all the jewelry you possess at one time.

Do not wear silver and gold together, unless they are combined to form a design.

If the sleeves of your gown are short, and you feel that a bracelet will break the length of the arm or make it more attractive, no doubt it will be just the right thing. If it does not really show pleasing improvement, do not wear it.

In wearing rings, make sure that they are in accord with the garments you wear and try to avoid burdening your fingers with them.

Earrings, too, merit consideration. Sometimes they enhance a costume, emphasize a completeness of toilet that is pleasing; at other times they are so out of place as to appear almost barbaric.

It is not uncommon to see a young woman wearing all at one time a watch pinned to her blouse, several rings, from one to three bracelets, and a string of beads. Such a sight tells you that she is not practicing the rule of elimination or applying the laws of harmonious dress to herself.

THE WEARING OF FLOWERS

Flowers, "exquisite creatures" that they are, are beautiful always; but there are some cases where certain flowers, especially when worn by individuals, are more beautiful than others and a certain combination of flowers is more pleasing and expresses more individuality than another.

A young woman for whom I have the greatest admiration always plans the most unique color schemes in flowers that it has ever been my pleasure to see. It may be one rose in a vase or one rose on a gown, but it is just the right rose in size and color in exactly the right place, and it is more effective than a dozen would be when incorrectly used.

Once I saw this woman, whose eyes are as dark as night itself and whose hair is a very dark and beautiful brown, dressed in a dark-brown velvet gown simple in line, with just a plain piece of real lace in cream color at the neck coming down in a long line in the front. At the waist line, she wore one American Beauty rose with three green leaves. I wish you could picture how the long stem of the rose accentuated the long line of the collar and how the bit of color supplied that delightful touch which made the frock appear far above the ordinary.

If you are small in stature, trim in figure, and attractive in face, you can wear sweetheart roses, Killarney roses, rosebuds, lilies of the valley, or any exquisite little bouquet made of dainty flowers. But if you are large in stature, dignified in posture, you should be very careful to wear exactly the right flower of exactly the right size in exactly the right place.

I know a tall girl who wears tobacco brown a very great deal. One time you will see her, probably at an afternoon function, wearing a corsage bouquet of violets, in the center of which she has placed a beautiful marigold, thus giving just the life to the costume that the purple of the violets fail to give. Again you may see her at a fashion opening or a luncheon with one beautiful yellow chrysanthemum on her brown tailored suit. One thing, though, I have always noticed is that no matter what color of flower she wears, she has just a harmonizing fleck of the "yellow-gold" to enchance the beauty of the brown of her costume.

One day I saw a beautiful one-piece gown in a select shop. It was a reseda-green crêpe. The lines were as unpretentious as could be, but at the left-side front was a large fawn-brown velvet-and-linen rose with a long dark-green stem, the rose itself measuring possibly three and one-half inches in diameter. Peeking out were three little buds having a bit of chamois color, and at the neck was a collar of chamois color. The gown was wonderful. Why? Because it was simple, and each color was exquisitely in tune with the other.

Many beautiful color effects can be produced with artificial flowers, and such flowers are so simple and easy to make from bits of silk and ribbon and frequently so reasonable in price at the stores that when they are in fashion, you, as well as every other woman, may, if you choose, possess a suitable bouquet for every gown or suit.

But you must exercise care in selecting just the right color, just the right size, and just the right number for your bouquet. Sometimes, one wee bud or blossom is all that is necessary.

One time I saw a large woman with a beautiful beaver coat wearing one tiny white rose near her face, on the lapel. It was placed correctly and was of a suitable size to soften the coat around the face and give a desirable individual touch.

A prominent business woman of my acquaintance who wears severely tailored frocks —usually a conventional blue serge—always uses a little stiff tailored rose or bud of some kind to lend color to her costume. She usually wears long white collars, and at the belt or on the shoulder she has a rose of very dark red— darker than the American Beauty—and sometimes this is backed up with a silver metal cloth, giving a stiff little flower that is in keeping with the tailored costume, but with just the touch of color that she feels she needs.

In wearing flowers, remember that some flowers, such as the old-fashioned garden flowers, are appropriate for summer dresses. Chrysanthemums, violets, and asters are appropriate to wear with suits and tailored garments. Orchids frequently are worn with suits, but they are not considered absolutely in good taste because of their frailty. For this reason, they are more frequently desired for wear with a beautiful evening gown or an afternoon frock. There are times, however, when orchids are beautiful with a suit. I remember of having seen a lavender orchid corsage bouquet worn with an exquisite gray velvet suit, not slate-gray nor mouse-gray, but an in-between gray, and it was just the right thing for that particular suit.

A GUIDE TO CORRECT DRESS FOR BUSINESS, OUTING, AND THE HOME—SPRING SEASON

Purpose	Dress	Hat	Coat	Gloves	Shoes	Accessories
Business, shopping, or walking.	One-piece dress of silk or wool, or blouse and separate skirt, semitailored; walking length.	Preferably close fitting; never extremely large; simple in effect.	Suit or light-weight cloak of becoming length, semitailored or strictly tailored and preferably of subdued color.	Rather heavy kid or fabric suede; tan, or to match suit.	High; medium weight; tan or black; lace or button; heels of medium height and size; walking shoes preferred.	Medium size bag, or pocketbook; preferably black or medium dark color.
Traveling.	Same as above.	Same as above.	Same as above.	Same as above.	Same as above.	Close-fitting veil and necessary traveling bag.
Motoring or outing.	Cloth suit with short skirt, semitailored; silk blouse and tailored skirt or one-piece dress of wool.	Very simple and close fitting; of soft felt, silk, leather, or kid.	Cravenette, flannel, or khaki; loose, long, or three-quarter length.	Tan cape, dogskin, or chamois.	High or low; low, firm heels; tan or black.	Change purse, vanity bag, and chiffon or silk mull veil.
Church, club meeting, or informal luncheon.	One-piece light-weight dress, or skirt to match jacket, with matching silk or light-lace, net, or chiffon blouse.	Becoming and simply trimmed, but more elegant than for business wear.	Suit or medium light-weight semitailored coat, of cloth or silk.	White kid, or to match suit.	High or low; plain kid or patent leather.	Small change purse; for elderly woman, silk or crocheted bag, in black or dark color, to hold purse, fan, and eye glasses.
Morning at home.	Simple washable dress or washable skirt and separate waist.	Hat to match garden frock of linen or rep.		Garden—leather or rubber.	Comfortable; high or low; black or tan.	Apron or cap, if work demands them.
Morning as a guest.	White washable skirt and separate waist, or pretty wash dress.		Knit sweater, or sport coat of wool or crash.		Same as above, or white or tan sport shoes.	Small work apron.
Afternoon at home.	Separate washable skirt and waist; simple one-piece dress.				Simple; good taste; black or colored shoes or slippers.	Small afternoon apron.
Afternoon as a guest.	One-piece dress of wool or silk; or white washable separate skirt and waist.				Same as for afternoon at home.	
Evening at home.	Same as afternoon; pretty silk for special occasions.				Same as for afternoon.	
Evening as a guest.	Same as for afternoon; or semievening or formal evening dress for special occasions, party, theater, or dance.			Long white or light-colored; silk or kid.	Black patent leather, or kid or satin to match dress.	Fan; scarf.

A GUIDE TO CORRECT DRESS FOR BUSINESS, OUTING, AND THE HOME—SUMMER SEASON

Purpose	Dress	Hat	Coat	Gloves	Shoes	Accessories
Business, shopping, or walking.	Light-weight wool or linen suit, with washable blouse; tailored linen, cotton, or washable silk dress.	Medium size; straw, or soft stitched fabric hat.	Unlined; three-quarter length, or shorter.	Washable; silk, lisle, or cotton.	High or low; black or tan; heels of medium size and height.	Medium size bag or pocketbook of fabric or leather; in black or colors.
Traveling.	Same as above.	Same as above.	Same as above.	Same as above.	Same as above.	Veil, umbrella, and traveling bag; rug and cushion, if necessary.
Motoring.	Dark silk or washable one-piece dress, or shirtwaist and suit.	Close-fitting fabric, straw hat or bonnet, or one of leather.	Medium-weight rainproof; three-quarter or full length.	Washable cotton, kid, or chamois.	Same as above.	Veil, goggles, and fitted toilet bag or case.
Outing.	Same as for motoring.	Same as for motoring.	Same as for motoring, or sweater.	Same as for motoring.	Same as above, or white canvas or suède.	Parasol; walking stick.
Church, club meeting, or informal luncheon.	Dressy silk or fine cotton gown; silk suit, with a lace or chiffon waist.	Attractive, dressy hat, trimmed in any style and material that is becoming and comfortable.	Silk, satin, or fine light-weight cloth; three-quarter length or longer.	White, lisle, silk, or kid.	High or low; black, or to match suit or dress.	Fancy bag or pocketbook; fan; parasol.
Morning at home.	Simplest cotton one-piece dress.	Garden hat or bonnet.	Garden smock.		High or low; black, tan, or white.	
Morning as a guest.	Same as above, or white waist and skirt.	Same as above.	Same as above.		Same as above.	
Afternoon at home.	Same as for spring.	Same as for spring.			Same as for spring.	Same as for spring.
Afternoon as a guest.	One-piece dress of washable material, or white waist and skirt.	Same as for spring.			Same as for spring.	
Evening at home.	Sheer white or colored cotton, lace-trimmed dress.				Same as for spring.	
Evening as a guest.	Dressy white or colored cotton, attractively trimmed; thin silk, chiffon, lace, or net for special occasions.		Becoming, easy to slip on wrap of silk, voile, or similar wool fabric.	White; silk or kid.	Same as for spring.	Fan; scarf.

A GUIDE TO CORRECT DRESS FOR BUSINESS, OUTING, AND THE HOME
AUTUMN AND WINTER SEASONS

Purpose	Dress	Hat	Coat	Gloves	Shoes	Accessories
Business, shopping, or walking.	Serge, gabardine, broadcloth, or poplin one-piece dress or suit with matching or washable blouses	Small; becoming; felt, fabric, or velvet.	Easy fitting; three-quarter length, or longer; cheviot, broadcloth, or fabrics of similar weight; raincoat.	Kid, castor, or heavy fabric.	High; tan or black; heels of medium size and height. Rubbers.	Pocketbook or bag; silk muffler; furs; umbrella.
Traveling.	Same as above.	Same as above.	Same as above.	Same as above.	Same as above.	Same as above, with traveling bag, rug, and cushion, if necessary or desired.
Motoring or outing.	Plain-cloth one-piece dress, or heavy suit with separate waist.	Small; close-fitting; felt, fabric, leather, or kid.	Same as above.	Same as above.	Same as above.	Same as for business or shopping, without umbrella.
Church, club meeting, or informal lunch.	Cloth or velvet suit, with matching waist; dress of silk, velvet, or combination of silk and cloth.	Becoming trimmed hat; felt, velvet, or silk.	Cloth, velvet, or fur, in any becoming and fashionable length.	White, black, or matching kid.	High; black, plain, or patent leather; kid or cloth top.	Small bag or coin purse; face veil; fan.
Morning at home.	Heavy cotton dress, or washable waist and skirt.				High or low; black or tan.	Work apron.
Morning as a guest.	Simple cloth or cotton dress, or separate waist and skirt.				Same as for morning at home.	
Afternoon at home.	Attractive cloth or cotton dress; shirtwaist and skirt.				Same as for spring and summer.	Small afternoon apron.
Afternoon as a guest.	Rather dressy cloth or cotton dress; fancy blouse and separate skirt.	Becoming; felt, silk, or velvet.			Same as for spring and summer.	
Evening at home.	Same as afternoon; or pretty silk, if entertaining.				Black or colored kid slippers.	
Evening as a guest.	Same as afternoon; for special occasions, evening dress of silk, net, lace, chiffon, or fine fancy cotton.	Becoming and tastefully trimmed silk or chiffon hood.	Cloth or velvet wrap, or fur coat.	Long or short; white or matching kid.	Black or colored kid or satin slippers.	Fan; scarf; carriage slippers.

A GUIDE TO CORRECT DRESS FOR SPECIAL FUNCTIONS—ALL SEASONS

Purpose	Gown	Head Dress	Wrap	Gloves	Shoes	Accessories
Formal luncheon, day wedding, calling, or afternoon tea.	Dressy suit of fine cloth, silk, or velvet with matching waist; or, rather elaborate dress of cloth or silk or a combination of chiffon and silk or silk and cloth, probably white at the neck.	Becoming, dressy hat, of any fashionable size or shape.	Three-quarter or longer; silk, cloth, or velvet.	White kid; long or short, as the sleeves require.	Black, bronze, or matching kid; high or low.	Small, fancy bag; fan; face veil.
Informal dinner at home.	Any becoming silk or cotton gown.				Same as above.	
Informal dinner at restaurant or hotel.	Same as for formal luncheon, etc.	Same as above.	Practically same as above.	Practically same as above.	Practically same as above.	Practically same as above.
Formal dinner at home.	Simple, but becoming, evening dress.				Same as above.	Fan.
Formal dinner at restaurant or hotel.	Evening gown, slightly low in neck, or as for formal occasions; any style and color that is becoming.	No hat.	Silk or cloth coat or wrap.	White kid; long.	Kid or satin, to match gown.	Fan; scarf; opera bag.
Informal theater, concert, or lecture.	Practically same as for formal luncheon, etc.	Practically same as for formal luncheon, etc.	Practically same as for formal luncheon, etc.	Practically same as for formal luncheon, etc.	Practically same as for formal luncheon, etc.	Practically same as for formal luncheon, etc.
Formal theater, concert, or lecture.	Practically same as for formal dinner at restaurant.	Practically same as for formal dinner at restaurant.	Practically same as for formal dinner at restaurant.	Practically same as for formal dinner at restaurant.	Practically same as for formal dinner at restaurant.	Practically same as for formal dinner at restaurant.
Informal evening party.	Any simple, attractive, semievening dress of silk, net, lace, etc.		Cloth or silk.	White or color to match; silk or kid.	Black, bronze, or matching satin or kid slippers.	Scarf; fan; slipper bag.
Formal evening party.	Décolleté; black, white, or color; in silk, net, lace, or chiffon; may be very plain, if of handsome fabric, or trimmed.	Fancy comb. Matrons may wear feather ornament; girls, flowers, tulle, or ribbon.	Cloth or silk.	White or color to match; kid.	Same as above.	Same as above.
Formal ball or opera.	Practically same as above.	Practically same as above.	Practically same as above.	Practically same as above.	Practically same as above.	Practically same as above.

So that you may form a more definite idea of what may be worn to advantage for business and outing and in the home, as well as what may be worn at special functions, I have arranged several guides in the form of tables. These tables are intended simply to assist you in planning for yourself, and if you refer to them persistently and interpret their contents correctly you will derive much benefit from them.

The one relating to special functions is in the form of an all-season chart, because there is not a great difference between the several types of garments. In winter, heavier-weight materials and more brilliant colors are used than in spring and summer; also, more garments are provided, because, as a rule, there is more social life in the autumn and winter seasons.

What you should wear to the theater depends largely on the seat you are to occupy. It is perfectly correct to wear the same garments and accessories as are provided for Informal Theater if a theater box is to be occupied; and it is very much better taste to do so if the trip to the theater is not made in a private conveyance.

Rather than slavishly follow the prevailing mode, you will find that the most beautiful, and decidedly the most practical, evening clothes are those which are designed to suit you, because they can be used for more than one season.

Formal dress should depend on the beauty of fabric and color, rather than on intricate style. Informal evening dress is best when made of inexpensive fabrics, with more regard to design, for such garments are subject to harder usage than the more formal evening gowns, and as they are worn oftener they have shorter life.

If your circumstances are moderate, one evening wrap of conservative design, color, and fabric should serve you at least two years, and for all seasons except summer.

Garments of unlined silk or of knitted or crocheted silk or wool are acceptable for summer.

If you are not accustomed to attending many formal affairs and attend more afternoon than evening functions, you should select an afternoon coat of neutral tone or very dark shade, and a style and fabric equally suitable for afternoon and evening wear.

Goldwyn Pictures   *Photo by White*

GERALDINE FARRAR

**Whose individuality seems always to demand clothes extraordinaire—
clothes that express the elegance of opera**

CULTIVATING INTELLIGENCE IN DRESS

I am giving here a few suggestions that, although seemingly commonplace, are of such practical value that they must be considered where appropriate or harmonious dress is concerned.

A dress may be ever so beautiful, yet, unless the individuality of the wearer and the accessories of the costume are in harmony with it, it will undoubtedly prove to be an expensive failure. Some women fail to realize the importance of this detail, thinking that if their frock is attractive the matter is ended, whereas an attractive frock is only one essential of good dress.

It would seem that, in a general way at least, nearly all women know that there is a law of eternal fitness in dress; yet not all have the taste and fine discrimination to apply the law unto themselves, few take the care that they should in selecting material suitable for certain occasions, and fewer still have any appreciation of color and style in design unless they are specially trained in this direction.

It is true that no woman should wear materials of a color, design, or fashion that will in any way tend to exaggerate any marked characteristics or pecularities she may possess.

On the other hand, beauty of form and feature is generally sufficiently apparent not to necessitate calling attention to it by wearing garments that overemphasize these good qualities. Rather, an effort should be made to preserve the naturalness of these gifts and to show them in their greatest simplicity without making them brazenly conspicuous.

To dress correctly, you must have regard for the three forces of nature, namely, size, motion, and attraction. There is a fitness of sentiment in dress that requires the exercise of care in the adaptation of style to the individual, holding ease, grace, and individuality as superior to all other considerations, and remembering always that beauty of form in dress is produced by the artistic combination of graceful curves growing out of each other, the lesser from the greater, the harmonious application of trimming, and the correct combination of colors, all of which tend to produce a oneness of effect that is pleasing to the eye and that gives poise and dignity to the wearer.

In material, design, and the arrangement of its parts, the main structure of a dress should be free from all unnecessary additions that will in any way interfere with its beauty of outline or gracefulness. Accessories should

be judiciously applied, as if growing from the most dominant parts or lines of a costume and thus emphasizing them. If this thought is made to prevail throughout the trimming of a garment, it is possible to add force to the leading lines and develop a very harmonious display of coloring or line that will tastefully relieve any monotony of effect that might be characteristic of a severely plain dress.

As I have mentioned before, a piece of jewelry, such as a brooch or a necklace, will add much to the attractiveness of a bodice by giving tone or relieving plainness; yet these same ornaments may detract from the effect sought and even completely spoil it.

Effects produced by harmony are much more pleasing and powerful than those produced by exaggerations, which at first shock and then oftentimes blunt one's appreciation of the purely artistic.

Women who have a strict regard for dress and ornament will avoid any inharmonious contrasts, and will never regard dress as a trivial or unimportant question. Dress is all important because it portrays character and individuality; therefore, to appear at your very best at all times, you must give due regard to appropriateness, comfort, gracefulness, and harmony.

To many, "French woman" is just another way of saying "the well-dressed woman." We marvel at her becoming way of dressing, no matter what her station or what the occasion —how she seems to carry a harmonious thought throughout her costume; and, yet, knowing this characteristic of the French woman, that she does suggest that which all women strive for—a pleasing appearance—we neglect to follow as closely as we should the thought she inspires.

Some claim that to dress well is a natural gift, and, to an extent, this is true. Nevertheless, women who are born without that quality which is so elusive and hard to define, and which is commonly called *taste*, need not despair, for with patience, study, observation, and application a very good idea as to the correctness and appropriateness of garments can be acquired.

Some women enthuse over certain colors. They want them, they like to have them, and yet such colors may be the most trying of all colors for them. A woman possesses commendable control when she can deny herself the colors she likes best and wears those which are best suited to her type.

A good idea of the fitness of a color scheme in costume may be had from the following:

There were once two schoolgirls who looked very much alike. They were of the same size and had the same coloring and general outline of feature. The mother of one often wondered why her daughter did not look so well dressed as the other girl. So one day she asked permission from the mother of the girl who looked very smart and attractive, to copy her daughter's dresses, stating that she would use another color so that there would not seem to be such a sameness in the garments. The girl who appeared smart and attractive wore an entire suit that was in absolute harmony; her accessories, her shoes, her hat, her coat—all were in accord with her dress. Thus, one suit that she wore was simple in line and of smooth surface—brown material with a soft, cream blouse—and as accessories she wore a brown belt, brown gloves, brown shoes, and a cream-white straw hat trimmed with brown poppies. The other girl's mother, in her endeavor to have her daughter appear as attractive, duplicated this suit in blue, bought a light straw hat trimmed with red poppies, made blouses of various colors, and used gray gloves. Thus she ignored absolutely any thought of harmony, and while her daughter's things were more expensive they were not effective. They lacked distinctiveness—discrimination; they lacked the well-dressed woman's knowledge and expression of color harmony.

In such failures as this lies a very good lesson—in fact, one of the secrets of dressing becomingly.

In every case, you must have a definite idea as to the extent of your wardrobe when you attempt to replenish it. If you know that brown and blue are your most becoming colors, you should decide which of these is better suited to the occasion or to the season and stick to this color, and, if possible, have accessories to correspond.

This way of dressing will also prove very economical if it is adhered to closely, for one pair of shoes, one pair of gloves, and one hat will often suffice for many occasions.

If your purse will not permit of more than one complete costume and you find that tailored clothes fit into your needs best, stick to them. Do not change over to fluffy things and then try to combine plain and fluffy clothes and expect to get a harmonious effect.

An overelaborate hat will spoil a tailored street suit, as will also shoes that are meant for indoor or party wear. Heavy shoes are no more in keeping with an afternoon frock than are street gloves or a tailored hat.

A CLOTHES TRIUMPH

A physician with whom I am well acquainted—a capable, conscientious woman, skilled in her profession—had been so absorbed in her work that she never once considered the appropriateness of her clothing. This worked a handicap for her, because many people said that while she had demonstrated that she was a capable physician she was too frumpy in dress to impress one with her intelligence.

I like the doctor, and I appreciated her situation; also, I realized, when just hinting at the subject, that she, too, had been conscious of it for years.

She said, "I should like to be your patient and have you diagnose my case and plan clothes for me, just as I would diagnose your case and prescribe for you."

I agreed and "prescribed" clothes that I felt suited her exactly. She was deeply interested, and with her full cooperation the task was delightful.

She was as elated as a child when her associates remarked about the improvement in her clothes, and she told me that in less than two months there was a marked difference in the attitude of people toward her. Even the nurses in the hospitals had more admiration for her.

She realized that her word had more weight, more authority, even in her own household, and remarked that people who had not asked for her services before had called her in to administer to them.

She called it her clothes triumph, and said, "I have always been able to see that a well body and a well mind could go a long way toward making a person successful, but I never realized for an instant what a great factor clothes are until I had this definite lesson."

The experience related occurred many years ago. This doctor is one of the best-dressed women in the prominent city in which she practices. She pays capable designers to plan her clothes, so that they fit her needs exactly, express her individuality, and are entirely in keeping with her position in her community.

Vintage Notions Monthly continues to share the work of Mary Brooks Picken and the Woman's Institute which inspired my book *Vintage Notions*. Although the Institute was founded 100 years ago, the treasure trove of lessons and stories are still relevant today and offer a blueprint for living a contented life.

If you enjoyed this issue of *Vintage Notions Monthly*, visit AmyBarickman.com for more of my curated collection of vintage content including patterns and books for needle and thread, inspiring fabric and textiles & free vintage art every Friday. Be sure to tune in to *Vintage Notions* episodes for a guided tour through my collection of sewing and fashion history, as well as modern projects inspired by my extensive library.

www.amybarickman.com

Find free images, inspiration and books for the sewing and needle arts!

www.indygojunction.com

Featuring digital & print patterns, books, tutorials, giveaways, project ideas, & more!

Subscribe to each of our eNewsletters to learn about new products, receive special offers, discounts, videos, and get a FREE eBook!

✉ f 📷 ⓟ 🐦 YouTube

Vintage Notions Monthly, Issue 14 (VN0202)

For wholesale ordering information contact Amy Barickman, LLC at 913.341.5559 or amyb@amybarickman.com, P.O. Box 30238, Kansas City, MO 64112

44851046R00040

Made in the USA
San Bernardino, CA
25 January 2017